Praise for *How to Audition for TV Commercials*

"Entertaining and well presented, this is a valuable resource for every commercial actor and would-be commercial actor. W.L.'s years of experience provide a behind-the-scenes look into areas that most actors will never have the opportunity to view unless, of course, they are close friends with or related to an agency creative or commercial director. And, W.L.'s love of the craft is apparent as he explains the many factors that come into play as an actor is considered for a role. Humorous and revealing, he has opened the door on those dirty little secrets hidden in a very mysterious process."—*Barbara E. Cline, Commercial Producer*

"This guide is a must-read for any actor professional or novice who is serious about working in commercials. W.L. has explained the unexplainable!"—*Michael Norman, Commercial Director*

"The best book I've read on how ad people like me choose actors like you for a part. Incredible insights on how to get the gig. If you think it's all about talent, performance, credentials or fairness, stick a fork in yourself, you're done."—*Howie Cohen, Chief Creative Officer, The Phelps Group*

D0710070

How to Audition for TV Commercials

How to
Audition
for TV
Commercials

From the
Ad Agency
Point of View

W. L. Jenkins

ALLWORTH PRESS
NEW YORK

© 2005 William L. Jenkins

08   07   06   05   04   5   4   3   2   1

Published by Allworth Press
An imprint of Allworth Communications, Inc.
10 East 23rd Street, New York, NY 10010

Cover design: Derek Bacchus

Cover photo: paulgodwin.com

Interior design: Mary Belibasakis

Page composition/typography: Integra Software Services, Pvt. Ltd., Pondicherry, India

ISBN: 1-58115-419-4

Library of Congress Cataloging-in-Publication Data

Jenkins, W. L. (William Lewis), 1949–
    How to audition for TV commercials: from the ad agency point of view / W.L. Jenkins.
        p. cm.
    Includes index.
    ISBN 1-58115-419-4 (pbk.)
1. Television broadcasting—Auditions.   2. Television acting—Vocational guidance.
3. Television advertising—Vocational guidance.   I. Title.

    PN1992.8.A3J38 2005
    792.02'8—dc22

                                                                2005009774

Printed in Canada

To Cora Lea.
My wife, my star, my forever friend.

"Success is going from failure to failure without loss of enthusiasm."

—Winston Churchill
(Obviously, Winston Churchill wasn't a commercial actor.)

Table of Contents

Prologue: The Other Side of the Room

There I am. Sitting on the other side of a hot, cramped little room that's lit up like a Wal-Mart, twitching uncomfortably in my seat, watching actor after actor come in to audition for one of my ad agency's TV commercials. Watching actors blow it. Watching people who remind me of myself years ago.

I don't want to see me come into the room anymore.

You see, I was once a professional actor and I worked at it for eight years. I've walked in your shoes. I understand what it's like to be an actor. I understand what it is like to go to a commercial audition, walk in, and become nervous, uncomfortable, and lost. What I didn't understand at the time was why that happened to me over and over.

I have a unique perspective your situation because I'm now an advertising creative director, and since starting in the business as a copywriter in Los Angeles in the mid-1980s, I've created a lot of TV commercials—and witnessed a zillion auditions. Time after time I've watched talented people come through the door and make stupid, avoidable mistakes. I see actors who are intimidated, unprepared, and don't know what to expect.

Whether you're an actor who wants to break into commercials, an actor who auditions but can't seem to get a lot of bookings, or a successful actor looking to stay competitive, you will find this book to be unique and helpful. Unlike other books about auditioning, this one is going to give you inside information about how to audition for TV commercials *from the ad agency point of view*. Like I said, I don't want to see me walk into the room anymore. I don't want to see you screw up, and believe it or not, ad agencies don't want you to fail, either. We absolutely need you to win. It's in our best interests to cast the right person, and it could certainly be you.

This is a book that understands actors, and it'll use familiar acting terminology, *but it's not a book about acting technique.* There are already hundreds of books about acting and plenty of commercial audition classes are accepting students, so I'll leave the craft stuff to you and your coach. It's not a book about how to break into commercials, or how to land an agent, or how headshots should look, either. No, what you'll learn here is some practical, useful information about what to expect, what to do, and *what not to do* when you go up to audition in front of a bunch of stressed-out advertising people who may want you in their TV commercial. It'll show you that there's a lot more going on with those people on the other side of the room than many actors realize. It'll show you how not to alienate them.

Alienate them? Yes. Actors say or do little things that may seem innocent, but they create negative impressions with the decision-makers sitting out there in the dark. Many actors don't take the time to do their homework on commercials, either, and that's not only unprofessional, it's a major turnoff. Most of the information in this book is just common sense. But if you could sit with me you'd be surprised how many times actors walk into an audition and throw common sense out the window. And along with common sense, out goes the respect of the agency and the director. Listen, you could give a so-so performance, but if there's something about you that the director likes, or there's something intelligent that you said or did, you could still find yourself in the running. On the other hand, even if you've given a good audition, if you come off as someone who doesn't have his head glued on, you're going to find yourself thinking, "You know, they should've called me by now!"—a lot.

Here's a small taste of some of the secrets you'll learn that'll help you keep your head in the right place:

○ How an ad agency works, and how commercials are created.

○ Understanding concepts.

○ The DNA of TV commercials.

○ How to really watch TV spots and use that knowledge to land parts.

- Directors' insights you can really use.

- What questions are appropriate to ask a casting director.

- What not to wear to an audition.

- How to "slate."

- How to read a script.

- How to understand a storyboard.

- What to do when things go wrong in the middle of your audition.

- The seven deadly sins actors make as soon as they walk into a callback.

- What an ad agency bases its casting decisions on.

- Ad agencies' criteria for choosing you for a part.

"*And*," as many ads shout, "*so much more!*"

You'll be surprised how behind-the-scenes information like this can give you an edge over other actors up for the same part as you. Because, as a commercial actor—more than in any other performing discipline—you need to be prepared for anything. You're walking into a very stressful situation where you're always going to cold-read in front of people who don't know the first thing about acting, and you realistically *have only two to three minutes to get a job*! So the point is, if you know how to put yourself in the best possible position to show off your acting abilities and focus under pressure, and know how to avoid making a bad impression by wasting the agency's and the director's time, you'll increase your chances of landing more bookings.

Are you ready? Because you're up next.

1 Setting the Bar High

In the eighties there was a very funny, successful Bay Area–theater director/actor named Doug Johnson who moved to L.A. and became an extremely successful commercial actor. You'd see him all over TV in all kinds of commercials, and, like all successful commercial actors, *he appeared mostly in small parts*: one-liners, a guy in a crowd who reacts to something off-camera, the snoring husband, a guy walking by a swimming pool who gets splashed—all kinds of little bits and stuff. (And every performance was golden, by the way.) Sadly, Doug isn't with us anymore, but if he was still here, I'm sure he'd tell you that if you treat every part as if it were a big one, you'll book lots of small ones. It's good advice because every part you read for is important—no matter how small—because it's a *job*. The key to being successful as a commercial actor over a long period of time is to work! work! work! by doing small parts. The secret is that you must treat every audition like it's a call for a big meaty part or a reoccurring character appearing in a long-running campaign. That's how you get the small ones.

So, with that thought squarely in mind, for the sake of getting the most out of this book, and as a way to cover all the bases, let's set the bar high and assume that *all* auditions are for major parts. If we base everything we do on the concept that each job is a big one, then eventually, you'll prepare for each audition with the energy that's required for a big endeavor. You'll be way ahead of the pack.

Let's take a look at commercials themselves, too.

Yes, sadly, when you turn on the TV you see a lot of crappy ads. All those horrid mattress spots and lowbrow local car ads annoy me, too, and they give a bad name to my profession, but, unfortunately, everybody goes out on calls for stuff like that. It's the real world. So, what should we do? Well, if we assume *here* that all the commercials you'll be auditioning for are crappy, then you may end up doing crappy work. So, to make your experience with this book worthwhile (and as part of my quest to eradicate bad commercials from the world), we'll also assume that all commercials are good ones—you know, funny, memorable, award-winning ads for big-time name brands that have big-time ad agencies and directors creating them. It just seems to make sense that approaching commercials with a positive mind-set here in this book, and especially in real-life, will elevate your thinking and your attitude and should help you be better prepared for most situations you'll encounter. The upside is that if you land a part standing next to that crazy furniture-store owner/spokesman with the bad toupee, hopefully, you'll be able to do us all a favor by applying what you've learned and making it a better commercial.

2 You versus the Business of Commercial Acting

I'm not going to quote all those labor statistics about how many people become actors every day and how just a few SAG actors make all the money. You're either someone who's deciding to be an actor and all the horror stories be damned, or you're somebody who's already made big sacrifices by becoming an actor; you're dedicated, and you know how difficult it can be. So do I, and I wish you the best.

In any case, you've been compelled to be an actor for various reasons, and I'll bet the most important are based on how acting makes you feel. It can be very rewarding in many personal ways. But there's something else. Aside from all your "burning desire," and the feeling that this is what you're destined to do, and the fact that performing gives you a rush that few people can comprehend, there's one thing that some of you have discovered. Whether you're enrolled in a drama curriculum in college, or drama school, or playing in little theater, or "big theatah," or taking scene-study classes, or whether you live in New York, L.A., or another large urban area and you're getting some TV and film roles—wherever you are—somewhere along the line you've come to the conclusion that, "You know what? I'm pretty damn good!" The applause, the better roles, the nods from your peers, and the hand on your shoulder from your acting teacher have validated this.

And, maybe you've discovered something extremely important— an element of your ability that will be your key to becoming a successful commercial actor.

You've discovered the incredible value of being.

CAN YOU "ACT?"

Hopefully, you've found out that there's no such thing as acting anymore, is there? Really, acting is the wrong term. "Acting" is *pretending*.

The new term is "being," and being is the pure state of existence that makes situations real. (For familiarity's sake, throughout this book, I'll use the words *act* or *acting*, but I really mean *being*.)

Oddly enough, you may look at a TV commercial and say, "Yeah, but that looks so *un*real." Don't think that way. Because honest to goodness, when it comes to TV commercials, ad agencies and directors want to see someone that we believe. We want somebody who *is* that person in the commercial.

> **TIP:** *Forget about acting. Ad agencies want to see people who are real.*

We don't want to see any pretend acting. Acting gets in the way of reality. We want people who are being.

"Right!" you say. "I'll buy that. I think I'm pretty good at being . . . um, er, acting."

Okay, you can act. But can you act in commercials?

Really. It's one thing to be able to clop around stage in a gown and bodice, all covered in makeup, and spew out iambic pentameter as nicely as Judi Dench and have people believe you, and it's another to look directly into a camera and talk about vaginal dryness and have people not only *believe* you, but go out and buy the product.

How do you find this out? Do yourself (and the world's ad agencies) a favor and take a commercial-acting or audition class. (Or, short of that, seek out some like-minded actors, tape some commercials, transcribe the action and the copy, and try out some moves on each other.)

> **TIP:** *The only way to find out if you can actually handle acting in commercials is to take commercial classes.*

By taking commercial classes, you'll have opportunities to determine if you can really be believable playing bizarre characters in the most twisted situations you can imagine. You'll learn if you can talk directly to a camera. You'll find out whether or not you can take a small piece of business that seems inherently inane and turn it into a moment that makes total sense. You'll discover whether or not you can take a line of dialogue or a simple gesture and make millions of people think you've got the answer to their most intimate problems. You'd be surprised how many actors come into an audition and can't do something as simple as take a walk across a room. It's true.

Actors who are relaxed, natural, and believable in totally unbelievable situations are actors we're interested in. If, however, in the classroom you discover that there are aspects of commercial acting that are too intimidating or just make you squeamishly uncomfortable, then you may want to make the decision to stick with acting experiences that are more enriching for you. You're not gonna make it in commercials, my friend, because believe it or not, we'll clearly see that you can't hack it right there on your initial audition tape. And you won't even get a callback.

GET SERIOUS

Okay, so you're not "acting." Or, at least you think you're not acting. You think you're good at *being*.

So, why do you want to do commercials?

I can see you scrunching up your face and coming up with some good reasons—which you probably have. But a lot of actors want to do commercials for the wrong reasons. And, just like a bad poker player who "tells" the other players he's bluffing by nervously scratching his ear or lighting a cigarette, when these actors appear on tape or in the studio, they show us that they're just fooling, too.

Here's where they're coming from:

Many actors think that a "look" and a fair amount of talent is all they need to walk right in and start working.

Some actors go out on calls thinking they'll pick up a little work even while feeling deep down inside that working in commercials is "slumming." Commercials are beneath them, not as pure as film, or, especially, "theatah." "Well, it isn't *art*," as some holier-than-thou once said.

Both of these attitudes tie into the biggest misconception of all: Commercials look easy to do. No. They look like *easy money*. Actors (and ordinary folk) sit at home on the couch watching commercials and they see somebody react or smile or take a swig of cola or whatever and they say, "Come on, it's gotta be a piece of cake. A couple of minute's work, and wait for the checks to roll in. Ka-ching!"

Here's something that my old friend, Troy Evans, told me. Troy started acting in a little theater in Montana over thirty years ago and has been hard at work ever since. He's never given up, and the result has been long-running roles on shows like *China Beach* and *ER*, dozens of movies playing people like John Travolta's friend in *Michael,* and a good share of commercials along the way.

"People ask me this maybe twenty-five times a year, 'Aren't you that guy on *ER*? That actor?' And I say, 'Yes, I am.' Then, they ask, 'How'd you get in on that?' People don't view it as something you *do*, they view it as something you *get in on*. Like, how did Barry Bonds get *in on* baseball! Well, he worked his ass off from the time he was a little kid, and he continues to."

> **TIP:** *If you think this looks like an easy way to make money, you don't have a prayer in this business.*

Actors who are guided by that kind of thinking aren't really offending anyone. But they're hurting their chances for success because what they're really saying is that they aren't *serious* about this business. Too bad, because commercials attract a lot of highly motivated people, and people who take it seriously get the bookings. That's not to say that you shouldn't pursue—other acting avenues while you try to work in commercials—everybody does but if you're going to do this, DO IT FOR KEEPS. Ladies and gentlemen, there's a lot at stake when you walk into that audition studio. Yes, you could book a job that pays you $35,000. That's the kind of high-altitude money that can give you a nosebleed. You could book a job that pays much less—say, a couple of car payments' worth. That's good, too. Or, you could book a part that gets you noticed. . . .

"Yeah, yeah, yeah," you're thinking. "Excuse me. Time out. The money and everything aside, all I'm doing is just coming in to read for a part, right?"

Hmm. Well, yes, but if you think that's all there is to it, then you're missing out on an important consideration that leaves so many actors wondering why they're not getting anywhere. There's something else at stake that many actors don't open their eyes to:

The people who sit back there in the dark on the opposite side of the room.

You must take a look at it from the *ad agency's* side. We're responsible for spending $100,000 or $250,000 or $1,000,000 *or more* of our clients' money for *one* thirty-second TV commercial, solely for the purpose of selling something of theirs. That's our job. The cost, and, therefore, the agency's responsibility, creates huge pressure on us to succeed. Understandably, we take this very seriously. And if you come in and you're not as serious as we are, *then we don't want you!* If you're not serious, believe me, we can see it and smell it. Just like sitting across the table from the bad poker player who "tells," we can spot someone with a half-assed attitude the minute they appear on the tape of the initial call.

> **TIP:** *Agency people and directors can usually spot the people who don't take commercials seriously.*

There's another thing you should know up front: Most advertising people haven't been in the entertainment business. They don't talk your language. They don't have an appreciation for your craft or what it's like to be an actor, and, therefore, they're not going to treat you with the understanding that you may be used to. They don't make traditional casting decisions. In their minds, the final decision between you and another talented actor who looks just as right for the part as you do may not be about your being right for the part at all. It may come down to, "Are you a person we want to work with?" An actor who seems to be taking the situation lightly isn't somebody we want to work with.

> **TIP:** *Most agency people don't appreciate the task of acting and the vagaries of the entertainment business.*

Another huge, snarling enemy of casting decisions is time. Not the thirty-second time frame of a TV spot (we'll get to that), but the time it takes to produce those thirty seconds. The production pace for a commercial is so insanely *fast* you'd think you should wear a helmet. That's why auditioning for a commercial is a much different experience than auditioning for theater, film, or television. The timeframe, starting from the agency's initial preproduction meeting with the director, through the casting process to the end of the shoot, may take only two weeks, or less! Now you can see the tight deadline the agency, the director, and the production people are up against. Tight deadlines call for fast decisions. Tight deadlines make for a crowd of uptight people sitting in a hot little room all day—people that you're going to perform in front of.

Sure, you may be one of those people who gets lucky and lands some work. It happens. But if your motivation comes purely from the idea that this looks like an easy way to make a few bucks, then you won't last very long. Some of you reading this book already understand that even though commercial acting is a bear, you've made a commitment to becoming successful. That's because you've also realized that *what happens in that audition studio is really more important than what happens in the commercial.* You've been able to separate the phony life you see in the commercial on TV from the awesome, sweaty reality of the audition. Never forget that what you see on the air is a finished product. The hardest part—the most important part—is getting the job.

> **TIP:** *The impression you make in the audition studio is more important than what you'll actually end up doing in the commercial.*

I'll let you in on a little secret. Those three idiotic opinions at the top of this section were mine when I was acting, and they killed me. I didn't realize how important it was to have a serious attitude until many years later, and then it was too late. I should have listened to Troy.

THE 20 PERCENT—WHY SOME ACTORS WORK AND MOST OTHERS DON'T

I can hear some of you. "Hold on," you're saying, "I'm serious. I'm committed. I'm just not . . . um . . . booking jobs."

Well, all right. You say you're serious and dedicated, good. You say you've got the fire, good. But why are you coming up dry? Maybe you're part of the 80 percent.

The who?

The 80 percent of people who come in to audition who have no clue how to audition for commercials. Ask any casting director and they'll tell you that no matter how serious actors are, 80 percent don't know what they're doing. It's obviously true. Time after time during casting sessions, some agency person will be reviewing audition tapes, stop, look up to heaven, and ask, "Why are they sending us these weenies!?"

Listen to this conversation I recently had with Mardel Monet, an old buddy of mine who's a senior art director at a major L.A. agency. His main job is to create commercials and ride herd on their production. He creates miles of commercials. We were talking about his latest project and, apparently, it was a bear to cast because he said, "Man, it's so hard to find good talent in this town! People come in and they're just clueless!" He was obviously frustrated, of course, because he knows L.A. is filled with good people. Sometimes, they're just hard to find. I asked him if maybe some of them didn't understand what was going on in the commercial and he said, "It's pretty obvious when people don't do their homework. We were just casting for a girl who's just supposed to give a look, you know, react for a two second shot, and *nobody could do it*. They don't seem to understand that good commercial acting is harder than it looks."

> **TIP**: *Eighty percent of the people who come into the studio don't have a clue how to audition for commercials.*

Eighty percent. Hmmm, that means 20 percent are more likely to get all the bookings. They must be more serious, more *something* than you are, so what are they doing that you aren't?

Well, first of all, those 20 percent have made it their business to study commercials. They watch 'em and learn. They also know how they're created, how they're made, and who the players are that make things tick.

Those 20 percent understand that this isn't film or theater. It's *advertising*. Every character written into any TV commercial, directly or indirectly, has something to do with what's being *sold*. They know how they fit in with that program without actually being a salesperson.

They realize that commercial acting is more difficult because they're dealing with topics and ideas that most folks never really talk about. Movies and plays are about situations that people have actually been in. But talking about "new and improved Clorox?" Have you ever had a serious talk with anybody about new and improved Clorox? No. But commercial acting teachers can teach you a specific technique to be able to do this. Which brings up a point that bears repeating: To stay at your peak you need to constantly train with a commercial teacher. If you aren't in class, it's your ass.

The 20 percent know that the commercial audition process can be exhausting and complex, and they know how to deal with it. They know how to put themselves in the best possible position to show off their acting abilities and focus under pressure.

The 20 percent know that in order to work! work! work! they've got to be *prepared*. Even if you've never been on a commercial audition in your life, if you're prepared, you'll be more focused and less nervous. At the least, *you'll look like you're ready to go to work* when you walk into the room.

And finally—and this is absolutely key—the 20 percent know how to behave at an audition. Whether in person or on tape, successful commercial actors increase their chances of landing more bookings because they know how to avoid making bad impressions that waste the agency's and the director's time. Once again, they understand that what happens in the studio is more important than what actually happens in the commercial.

In my talks with casting directors about what they look for in an actor when he or she arrives at a call, veteran L.A. casting guru Dorothy

Kelly summed it up best. She looks for "A feeling of confidence. A feeling that the person is a professional. Someone who knows what they're doing so there's that certain bearing . . . that the person is in control."

This reassuring air of confidence can make a big difference in the way the people on our side of the room treat you. "Because," as Dorothy added, "ad agency people are insecure enough as it is."

③ It's Time for Your Close-Up

Before any commercial-casting director takes a look at you, you've got to take a hard look at yourself. Not just the way you look, but the real you. If acting is about finding the truth, then actors must find the truth in themselves. This can be hard for some people, but when it comes to acting in commercials, the truth often needs to be scrubbed clean and revealed. Can you handle the truth? Over the years I've found it good business to audition stand-up comics for certain roles. Those that learn how to drop their act and just *be* seem to do well. I think it's because they've gone through a process of stripping themselves down to find the essence of their comedy. In doing so, many of them find their true selves. This doesn't guarantee that they're all great actors, but their quest is a good lesson for everybody.

TAKING STOCK: WHO ARE YOU?

Probably the most liberating and identifying question that can be answered by immersing yourself in a commercial class is, "What makes me special? What do I have that no one else has?"

Everybody has a quality about them that people can define. What's yours?

Are you sophisticated?

A tomboy?

Cerebral?

Seductive?

European?

Hip?

Hip-hop?

Campy?

Urbane?

Geeky?

Infectious?

Brash?

Droll?

Authoritative?

Chic?

Country?

Whatever you are, it's something that makes you different from everyone else. In advertising, we call this the USP—the Unique Selling Proposition—and it's that singular thing that sets a product apart from every other one. Ad agencies ferret out that unique quality in a product or service, shine a spotlight on it, and use it to sell. You need to do the same thing. You need to take an honest appraisal of what it is about you—your essence, your special quality—that sets you apart from everyone else, and then you've got to recognize that the way you look and talk and stand and walk and dress is all a part of that essence. And in the end, when you can say, "This is me," then you've found your USP.

TIP: *You've got to find your USP.*

It used to be that people who appeared in TV ads were pretty much of the nonthreatening, good-looking "white-bread" variety. They were cast that way because advertisers believed that America aspired to be like those people. As times changed so did the people in commercials. Some bright bulb at an ad agency realized, "People are real! We need real people in our spots to reflect the real face of the consumer!" So they got real. Then things got realer and realer and realer. And today, especially with the phenomenon of "reality TV," characters are wilder, more unique, and more against type than ever. And it makes for a lot of fun.

This is where you come in. There's room in TV land for all kinds of people. People like you. The trick is to embrace your USP and use it to your advantage.

If there's anyone who's an authority on this subject, it's director Danny Levinson. Danny's built a solid reputation as a "people director" and sums it up this way: "Commercials are a visual medium, and so much of it, just by the nature of the beast, so much of it is the way you *look*. Yes, commercials have dialogue; yes, they have music; but in the end, they're a visual medium. You have to have confidence in yourself. I know it's a business that doesn't necessarily breed confidence, but that's why you have to be yourself."

> **TIP :** *Don't let the fact that you look "different" hold you back.*

It's wacky, but usually the thing you dislike about yourself is the thing that will get you jobs. So, be true to yourself. Love that big 'ol honkin' nose sitting on your face, or love that you're a wimp, or a ditz, or you look like a biker, or you have a squeaky voice, or come off as a snob, or *whatever* it is, because in this business those are attributes that make you unique. This is your look, your type, but most important, your *you*. Figure out your uniqueness. Embrace it. Then go out and market it. The commercial industry tends to pigeonhole types and you need to find your niche and work it, baby.

Hopefully, you'll come to understand one solidifying and gratifying fact that can keep you going when the chips don't fall your way. You can encourage yourself with the idea that, for all the people who go out there for parts, the one thing commercials don't have is *you*.

DO YOU KNOW WHAT YOU LOOK LIKE?

Bernard Hiller is a terrific actor who's booked his share of commercial gigs during his career and will continue to do so. (I first met him years ago when we cast him in a couple of fast-food spots.) He's not only a working actor, he's developed into a world-renowned acting teacher, teaching seminars in Rome, Paris, Moscow, and his Los Angeles studio. His methods are life-defining and intense. One of the most simple, yet astounding, exercises he asks of students is to have them bring in magazine ads featuring people who they think they look like. "Believe it or not," he says, "few people have a sense of who they look like." Someone who looks like George Clooney, for instance, will bring in pictures of Woody Allenish–looking guys. A woman will bring in pictures of ladies who look like Halle Berry when she really looks like Queen Latifah. The point of this exercise is that when you know who you look like, you're going to be much more comfortable with yourself. And that sense of true self will show on the audition tape.

Ask friends or relatives, "Who do you think I look like?" Try to get an honest answer. A close girlfriend could say to you, "Well, you remind me of Renée Zellweger." Or a buddy might think, "You're like Will Smith." That's good. But if somebody's really honest and has the guts to tell you, "When I look at you I see a middle-aged divorcée, tinted red hair, and an annoying nasal voice, who gives me the impression that she's seen it all," well, now you're on to something.

It's easy to lose sight of yourself in other ways, too. One of the things that hindered me as an actor was that I got so hung up *on who I thought I wanted people to think I was* that I forgot *who I* was.

I wish I'd truly understood that everyone is, in their own right, a character. Never forget that you're uniquely yourself. Jack Nicholson has been quoted as saying that 85 percent of himself is exactly like the character he's portraying, and isolating the other 15 percent and deciding how to act it is how he begins his character analysis.

TIP: *Don't forget who you are.*

LOOK IN THE MIRROR

This may sound tough, but you must be acutely aware of anything physically negative about yourself that's ghastly. If you have a physical attribute that could turn people off, agency and production people could get turned off, too. Agencies get notoriously picky about appearance because the talent on that TV screen in your living room *represents our client*. So, you have to be honest with yourself and determine whether your physical appearance could be detrimental, and if so, ask yourself if it's worth correcting.

Finally, the way you take care of yourself—your grooming—can send some strong signals, too. If you come into an audition looking like shit, well, that's what kind of an actor we may think you are.

BE HONEST

Can you tap dance? I mean really Gregory Hines–caliber tap? Can you really play tennis? Cast a fly rod? Do a cartwheel? Chug a twelve-ounce can of soda without stopping?

Are you a vegetarian? Antifur? Allergic to cats? Are you blind without your glasses?

Over time, you're going to be presented with a smorgasbord of lifestyle situations to audition for. You have to be honest about your ability to do what's asked. Be up front if you have a physical limitation that could prevent you from performing, or you have a personal aversion to certain foods, or there are issues concerning political correctness that make you go all snarky. If you find yourself in any situation where you have doubts or can't actually do what's required, turn down the audition, dammit, because if you come in and try and fake it, you'll be up to your neck in pissed-off ad agency people and casting directors. What's worse, many people in the business have long memories, and even though you may be a terrific actor, they may remember your one gaffe.

Don't do it unless you can really do it.

> **TIP:** *Don't get caught trying to pull off something you can't really do.*

Here's an example: When casting a burger commercial, we saw a guy on tape who was a good actor and delivered a good performance. But instead of taking a big chompin' bite out of the pretend burger (represented by a piece of bread at the session), he started doing this sort of dainty nibbling thing, like he was afraid of the bread. Well, we liked him enough to call him back, figuring that the director could get him to take a nice big chomp at the audition. But he did the same thing. And when the director asked him why he wouldn't bite a burger like normal, the actor said, "Oh, I could never do that, *I'm a vegetarian.*" WHAT? Do you know those trap doors you see in movies that open with a secret button? I wished I had that button. What was this guy thinking? Can you imagine if somehow the director got him to bite a piece of bread, we hired him, and we found out on the set that he couldn't eat a real burger? Whoa!

Also, *don't do it if your heart's not in it.* Director George Roux relates this incident: "Part of the reason I love actors is because they all seem so fearless, and that's what I expect out of them, to trust me enough to make them know that I'm not going to make them look like an idiot.

"One time we had a spot where a guy was sneaking looks at all his Christmas packages hidden under the bed. He had to take the lid off and react and look almost silly and childlike. One actor came in and did a really nice job, so we hired him. Got him on the set and I couldn't get him to do anything! Finally, I just said, 'Stop, let's take a break,' and I took him aside and asked him what was going on. He said, 'Well, I don't want to look silly.' And I said, 'You took the job, it's supposed to be silly, it's supposed to be fun. I'm not trying to make you look like an idiot, I'm supposed to make you look childlike and, y'know, *fun*.' And, d'you know what? He'd just decided it was bad for his *image* to be silly! So we had some stronger words, and finally I got a performance out of him. But I said, 'This is really bad news if you're gonna do this in your career. If you don't want the job, don't take the job.'

"This guy thought I was going to make him look like a boob and he just wasn't going to do it, when in fact nothing had changed from either of his two auditions."

TIP: *Don't read for the part if you don't feel your heart's going to be in it.*

BE *REALLY* HONEST

Do you have *it*? You know what *it* is, don't you?

One day I was standing at the necktie counter at a Nordstrom out in the San Fernando Valley. It was one of those summer days in L.A. when it's so hot that everything seems to have a grayish-white cast to it, like ash. In an act of overcompensation, the store had the air conditioning turned up to "stun," and I really noticed how chilly it was. But as I perused the ties, I began to notice something else—a presence to my left, about ten feet away, that was very strong. It distracted me from the chill and the bright colors of the ties, and I looked up. There was a man shopping like everyone else in the icy cold store, but that man radiated *it*.

He was Harrison Ford.

If you've been landing good parts in plays or some TV, or let's just say people are somehow attracted to you, you probably have *it* and God bless you. But if you ain't got *it*, then don't kill yourself. Move on to something else.

> **TIP:** *If you don't have* it, *this could be a tougher business than you think.*

4 Advertising 101

How an Ad Agency Works, How Commercials
Are Created, and How You Can Benefit

If you bought a DVD player for the first time and you figured the only functions you'd need to know to make it operate were play, pause, and stop, you could get by with just those functions and watch movies. But you'd be missing the rich experience that the DVD player really offers. If you audition for TV commercials by just coming in and reading a part, well, that's the same as *not* knowing what all those buttons do on the DVD player.

Consider this chapter to be those extra buttons. It's very helpful to know the details about ad agencies so you can press the right buttons with agency people. It's also important for you to appreciate what these hardworking people have to deal with on a daily basis. (If you want to be a lion-tamer, it's a good idea to know about lions, right?)

Moreover, once you know how a commercial is created, once you know *why* certain elements are in there, you'll have a better ability to know *what* to do when you read for one.

Remember, this isn't Chekov. This isn't a Fox sitcom. This isn't an industrial.

It's advertising.

THE AD BIZ IN A NUTSHELL

"Advertising is like that crazy old aunt who lives in the little room upstairs in the attic. Everyone knows she's there, but nobody likes to talk about her."—W. L. Jenkins

For some reason, the ad business has always existed behind a veil of mystery and myth. Unlike a washer repairman, or a dentist, most people aren't quite sure about ad agency people or what they do. The old stereo-type is the cocky guy who has two martinis for lunch and then bangs out a couple of ads before quitting time, like Darrin Stephens from *Bewitched*. Nowadays, ad people are portrayed in movies and on TV like the cool yet outrageous creative director played by Tom Hanks in *Nothing in Common*, or the touchy-feely guys in *thirtysomething*—brilliant, witty people who work in really hip offices. People who can pull ideas out of thin air.

A lot of people think we have it easy, that it's a cushy job.

Bull.

The fact is, advertising is a cutthroat business where agencies spend a lot of time landing a client and, once they get one, spend the rest of their time trying not to lose it. The pressure to perform is relentless and the deadlines are never ending. It takes a thick skin to exist here, because, as in the entertainment business, you're only as good as your last hit show. Agency people are gifted, passionate, highly motivated (and often highly paid) professionals. They have the best sense of humor of any group of people I've ever been around save improv comedians. They are notoriously cynical. It's a business where award shows abound and the rewards for stardom are high, so it's no wonder you'll run into a lot of people with egos that rival Louis the Sun King's.

But if there's anything you should know about advertising people, it's this: In the pressure cooker of creating a TV commercial, events happen fast, time is precious, and the people on the front line—the art directors, copywriters, and producers—are the people who take the first hit when something goes wrong. They don't have much time to get things done, so the one thing that you don't want to do as an actor is waste their time at an audition. It makes them edgy and they lose their patience. You want them on your side.

As we go on, I'll show you the things to avoid that waste their time, and how to increase your chances for success. But first, let's take a ride on the back of a TV commercial.

> **TIP:** *One key to getting ahead is understanding the job of those agency people who sit on the other side of the room.*

CREATING A TV COMMERCIAL

On the surface, TV commercials, films, and television (episodic, sit-coms, etc.) all seem to be cut from the same cloth. Stories, characters, actions, and motivations are captured on film or video and edited into a cohesive piece, true—but the difference with TV commercials is that there are a lot of different *sales elements* at work. Don't ever forget that the main purpose of a commercial is to sell something, and so commercials are built upon such factors as the USP, the target market, brand personality, executional tone and manner, and other elements designed to drive the message home. This stuff is really the DNA of TV ads.

These elements can affect your performance, and knowing what they are can give you an edge when you come in to audition. We'll cover them all.

Some people (like my Mom) think that TV commercials just sort of magically pop up out of nowhere on TV, and I figure she's probably better off if I never tell her how commercials are created. But for someone like yourself, who uses background information as fuel for the creative process, it's going to be very helpful to get a feel for the development of a TV commercial, and along the way, grab some important elements that you can use.

So here follows a Cliffs Notes version of the life of a commercial, from its conception up to the point before it goes into production. You'll meet the main players and the roles they play, the process, and the essentials.

The Players

Occasionally, I'll talk with someone who mistakenly believes that advertisers themselves actually create all the advertising we see. In a few cases they do, and those companies maintain an "in-house" staff to handle the chores. With rare exceptions, in-house agencies do a miserable job. It's not hard to figure out why. The staff is just too close to the decision-makers above them. Their creativity, experimentation, and risk-taking are constantly stifled.

Smart advertisers know that in order to foster an atmosphere that keeps their marketing senses sharp, there must be separation between them and the idea people.

The Client

Towering above all stands the Almighty Client. The client is the company that hires the ad agency to advertise its products or services. Clients come in many sizes and ideologies, with the best being those who value the counsel of their agency and generally let them do what they do best. These are few and far between, however. Most clients are confused by advertising, yet they are meddlesome to a fault. Sometimes they make you wonder why they hired an agency in the first place, but since they're helping us keep the doors open and people employed, well, okay, we'll put up with it. We'd better. The client pays the bills and therefore has the final say in all matters pertaining to the advertising. The client is represented by its director of marketing (the DM), his or her support staff, and others such as the product manager or someone from sales. Next to the president or CEO of the company, the DM has the final say. (These folks are also commonly, collectively referred to as the Client.)

For the sake of this little demonstration, let's pretend that this client is MegaPhone, the nation's leading wireless provider. By and large they're a pretty good client because they "get it." MegaPhone's ad agency is Jenkins & Associates.

The Agency

Like all ad agencies, Jenkins & Associates is basically divided into two camps—the account side and the creative side, with important support personnel connected to each camp. The account people (who are also called "suits" because—you guessed it—they wear suits most of the time) are responsible for the day-to-day business between the agency and MegaPhone. They interpret the client's needs, point them towards ways to grow their business, and offer to spend their money in the most equitable way possible.

The other camp is called the creative team, or, in ad slang, "the creatives," partnered in teams of an art director (AD) and a copywriter (CW) who are valued for their collaborative visual and writing conceptual abilities. They report to a creative director (CD) whose experience and vision makes him the creative point person and decision-maker for the agency. Together they take the client's input that's been interpreted by the suits, and use that information to create the advertising.

TIP: *Most of the people you'll deal with are from the creative side of the agency.*

The Creative Process

One day, after a powwow with the MegaPhone director of marketing, the suits tell the creative director that the client wants to air a thirty-second TV spot. Now, you can't just go off willy-nilly and dream up a TV spot. It has to be built on a strong foundation. So, the first thing the two camps at the agency do is get together and hammer out two important documents that will provide the basis for the advertising and the guidelines for its execution. They are: a strategy statement, which lays out what's needed (the objective) and how to achieve it; and a creative brief, which describes how to fulfill the strategy from a creative standpoint. When these documents are satisfactory to the agency, the suits soon present them to the MegaPhone DM and his related personnel.

Once the agency gets client approval on the strategy and the creative brief, the creative director meets with his art director/copywriter team to give them the assignment. It's the team's job to look at the creative brief and dream up concepts for the TV spot.

Now, this creative brief, this document, is the life-spring of the creative process. It contains key guidelines that will not only have a great effect on how the commercial is created and produced, *it will also have a direct bearing on what you do when you come in to audition in a couple of weeks.*

All briefs begin with a strategy statement that concisely spells out what product or service is being sold, and significantly, what the advertising needs to achieve. In this case, MegaPhone needs to attract new wireless business customers and they're offering a deal to get people to switch to them: no sign-up fee if you contract for their unlimited minutes package. Along with print and newspaper ads, they'll convey this message in a thirty-second TV spot. The brief spells out a production timeline with crucial deadlines along the way. These deadlines rule the lives of the creative team.

Now for the nitty-gritty.

Next, the brief includes a strong reminder about MegaPhone's *brand*. If you're a little hazy about what a brand is, here's an illustration I often use: You know who Jay Leno is, don't you? Okay, think about him for a moment.

. . . Jay Leno . . . Jay Leno.

Hmm. Did an image pop into your mind? A feeling? A reaction? Okay, that's your impression. Now, when I think of Jay Leno, what images and feelings does he conjure up for me? Well, let's see: Short guy, big chin, nasally voice, kind of feisty, *The Tonight Show* mystique, his cool set, Hollywood, politically cutting jokes, my sense of humor, Kevin Eubanks, jazzy theme song, my late-night habit, and so on. There's something else going on, too. Watching Jay Leno makes me feel, well, comfortable. Yeah, there's something comfortable about sitting in bed watching Leno. It's a good feeling. You probably have different images and feelings that the name Jay Leno conjures up for you. You may even have a negative image about Jay Leno, but the bottom line is that no matter what these impressions are, they constitute a *brand*. Jay Leno is a brand. If I say David Letterman, a whole different emotional picture forms for you and me (goofy laugh, gap-toothed grin, off-the-wall humor, New York attitude, etc.). He's a brand, too. What's more, the sum of everything about these individuals, and the way you and I respond to them, is a result of their *brand personality*. It's just the same for any brand of paper towels, running shoes, airline, or shampoo that's advertised—if the advertising is effective, they all have brand personalities, too.

MegaPhone's brand is actually written out as a statement, the main gist of which says: "MegaPhone is a very personable company with a 'do anything to help you' spirit." A more colorful, actionable, punchier way of putting it is to say that they're kind of spunky, which is actually *their* brand personality, their attitude. This human value of being spunky sets the *tone* and *manner* for all of their advertising, and so the spot will probably be executed utilizing their trademark "performing with a sense of humor under any circumstances" *concept* that is the strong, underlying theme of their entire ad campaign. The tone and manner directly influence the way the concept is brought to life. Its qualities will influence the way the entire commercial is produced, from choice of settings, the style of lighting, style of shooting, editing, sound effects, and even the fonts (typefaces) they'll use. (Fonts have a lot to do with our relationship to words. For instance, you can change the impact of a word simply by changing the font: Compare SPORTY versus **SPORTY**.)

Without question, music is one of the most potent tone and manner elements an advertiser can use to express its brand personality. Since music has such powerful meanings to us individually, it helps us identify with a brand in a one-to-one relationship. Why do you think so many advertisers have lifted pieces of popular songs as scores for their broadcast advertising? Because if you're a member of the target market that a particular ad is geared toward, a song you like will resonate with you. Why can't you get that stupid jingle out of your head? Because they want you to remember them. In MegaPhone's case, they incorporate music based on modern pop but don't directly lift a hit song and stick it into an ad.

MegaPhone's brand personality is also represented by a slogan (also called a "tag line" or a "position line"). Many advertisers have slogans and you're certainly familiar with them: Nike's "Just Do It" comes to mind as a slogan that was not only a perfect embodiment of their philosophy, but also a concept that resonated strongly with their target market of athletes and athletic wannabes. Simply put, a slogan should reinforce the advertiser's raison d'etre and at the same time reflect the target market's wants and needs. MegaPhone's slogan is "Good Call," and it's spoken at the end of their ads. Often you'll notice that many companies don't use a slogan. That's probably because they believe that the strength of their product and the way their commercials are executed say everything. And that works for them.

Tone and manner will have some bearing on the types of people who'll be cast to appear in the spot. But the most important factor that will influence casting is the group of people just mentioned above: The *target market* that the ads will be directed towards.

The target market is the group of people who are most inclined to purchase a product or service, and the brief succinctly delineates who they are. Over the years it's been discovered that people make choices for very specific reasons, and even the slightest breath of a new perception can influence their reason to continue to be loyal to a product they've been using—or try a new one. That's why, these days, target market determination has become a very exact science. And for the MegaPhone strategy it's been determined that the target is "heavy cellular users," *specifically* younger businesspeople on the go. So the spot will be crafted to speak directly to the lifestyle of that group of younger business people. And that determination will ultimately dictate the type of roles to be cast. If MegaPhone had decided to advertise some other deal to a different target they sell to, say upper-income teens who are addicted to their cell phones, that would be a different strategy requiring a different tone and manner. And different casting specs as well.

Tone and manner put the face of the advertiser on the commercial, and also provide an underlying tone of voice—a kind of ephemeral way the commercial (read: brand personality) speaks to the target market. As I pointed out, a target market needs to feel that the advertiser is on their wavelength so they'll feel more comfortable making a purchase choice. In the case of MegaPhone, young businesspeople on the go live in an entirely different world and use their cell phones for different reasons than a target market consisting of younger teens. The advertising can't talk to either target the same way, and the creative team knows this.

Brand personality. Target market. Tone and manner. These three advertising elements are the DNA of a brand, and therefore, elements that are at the heart of a commercial. But there's another, a fourth element that is crucial to the creation of a TV commercial. This element could make a difference in your ability to understand what is happening in the script. So, let's spend a minute or two with the concept of *concepts*.

Before We Go On, What's a Concept?

A concept is a potent idea that can be best expressed in a few words, but no more than a few sentences. A good concept will kick-start visual thinking. A good concept is loaded with *possibilities*.

We encounter concepts in all facets of life: Shopping malls. Democracy. Sport utility vehicles. The poor little rich kid. Theme parks. Bert Parks. Natural foods. Hip-hop. The new Hooters out by the lumberyard.

Yep, those are all concepts.

A concept for a play might be: A man who manufactures airplane parts cuts corners to save money. His son pilots a plane made with those parts, and he's killed when it crashes.

A concept for an episodic TV show might be: A New Jersey family has all the same ups and downs as any normal family. Except Dad is a mafia boss.

A movie concept might be: A crack in the space-time continuum transports a fast-talking theme-park maintenance man back to the days of knighthood. (If you want to get familiar with movie concepts, just go to your video rental store and read the movie synopsis on the back of any tape or DVD box. Like this one.)

Just like those examples, concepts for TV commercials should be entertaining, memorable, moving, and even provocative. They also have to be informative. But even more importantly, they absolutely must be designed to fulfill the ultimate goal: to sell something.

TIP: *Ultimately, all concepts for TV ads are vehicles used to sell something.*

For example: A winter's day, there's no snow to sled on and the grand-kids are bummed. Grandpa makes the kids believe they can magically *make it snow* just by drinking hot cocoa.

Or: You need to bank with us because our tellers are the friendliest people on the planet.

Or: A pizza chain says that your pizza is free if it's delivered later than thirty minutes from the time you ordered. People will do anything to make the delivery guy late.

Or: People will do anything for the great taste of (insert product name here).

Or: Life without: _____.

Here's one that ESPN used successfully for years: You'll never miss a moment of sports on ESPN because everyone connected with sports—players, coaches, even team mascots—lives full-time at the ESPN Sports Center headquarters.

A terrific example of a winning concept is the famous "Got Milk?" campaign from San Francisco agency Goodby/Silverstein. The tag line "Got Milk?" is actually a concept in itself because it's not only derived from a familiar everyday expression, it's a question that creates action: "What happens when you don't have any milk?" Now *that's* a concept that's just ripe for a zillion executions, and one of the first commercials they created set the tone for the great ones that followed.

The story was this: The scene takes place in the morning in an apartment kitchen with two young newlyweds at the breakfast table. The sleepy, smiling husband enters and his young wife sadly says to him, "You lied." Now, he thinks (and we think) she's accusing him of lying to her about some sort of secret he's been hiding. He's not sure what to do. He starts fishing around. The guy's so lame he not only spills the beans about his time in prison, he also tells her that the diamond engagement ring he gave her is really cubic zirconium. But all she really meant to say was that he'd lied about saving some milk for her. There wasn't any milk left in the fridge for her cereal, that's all. And that's what can happen when you don't have any milk.

Concept.

And a story with a beginning, a middle, and an end. Pretty simple and easy to understand. But how many times have you seen a commercial where the whole thing is comprised of seemingly unrelated shots and ideas? There doesn't appear to be much of a story or a plot line in commercials like those, *and sometimes there isn't.* You're always going to be confronted by scripts that don't track. What do you do then? The best thing is to roll up your sleeves and look for the concept.

There will always be one. Many times in commercials the concept *is* the story, and you can begin to get good at recognizing concepts when you study TV ads, which we'll deal with soon.

By the way, the milk spot used the common plot device of misconception. Naturally, there are all kinds of devices like "misconception," and they're actually cornerstones for the many *executional styles* of commercials we're familiar with. Later on we'll examine the various executional styles used to create TV ads, because you're going to encounter them in the audition studio, too.

TIP: *Every time you watch a TV commercial, try to figure out the concept. Then write it down. A good concept should be able to be described in one or two sentences.*

The Process Continues

Okay, let's return to our saga of the development of a TV commercial.

In order to develop concepts, the creatives use everything they experience in life as grist for their ideas: An overheard sentence in a supermarket, a scene from *Hawaiian Eye,* anime, the work of a cool new artist, The Cure, Fellini, cheesy seventies sitcoms, "My boyfriend said . . ." That's the great thing about being an art director or a copywriter: they're like anthropologists, and the world is one huge idea mine. They'll sit for hours tossing ideas back and forth. They'll dream up concepts in the shower, sitting on the train, sitting on the throne. They'll consult research about their target market to give them a better idea of how those people think, act, and talk. And they'll especially study the competitors' commercials to look for weaknesses and points of difference. You name it, they'll take whatever they can think of that's relevant to solving the puzzle, throw it into the creative Mix Master, pour it out, bake at 350° for an hour, and see if it measures up to the standards they've set based on the creative brief.

Time is one of their big considerations. Commercials can run ten, fifteen, thirty, sixty, and ninety seconds long, but the majority you see on the air are thirty seconds long. (They're called "30s.") But 30s aren't really 30s. To allow for the quarter-second fade-up at the beginning and the quarter-second fade-out at the end, a 30 is actually twenty-nine-and-a-half seconds long. This is the constrained little arena creatives are given to operate inside of. (It's the same tight box you'll be working in, too.) How long is twenty-nine-and-a-half seconds? If you read the previous six sentences comfortably out loud, that's roughly how much time it takes. As you can see, unlike a film or a play, where the authors have the luxury of letting words and action take whatever time they need to express the story, the creative team has to collapse time, distill thoughts, create visual magic, and deliver dialogue potent enough to make ideas instantly understandable—all in a few heartbeats. As a consequence, a commercial is actually a fairly fragile and elegant little piece of work.

> **TIP**: *Experiment with time. Develop an understanding of how long thirty seconds really feels.*

To continue: After a few days, some ideas begin to take shape for the team. Sometimes the nature of the advertiser's product, brand personality, and the underlying strategy dictates the executional style; sometimes it doesn't. But in this case the MegaPhone ads will fall into the category of Real-Life—albeit a real-life that has its reality pushed to the edge to make the ad fun and memorable.

The copywriter crafts some scripts (sometimes called "copy" or "ad copy") and the art director doodles some rough storyboards* (in ad slang also called "boards" or "visuals"), and as they get close to finalizing their ideas they'll also use a test to evaluate the probable effectiveness of the ads. It's a simple test, really, and all it does is ask five questions about each ad. If the commercial fails to answer "yes" to any question, then its life is in jeopardy.

* A storyboard is an illustrated version of the script. You'll learn about them in chapter 8.

The creative team wants to know, "Is this ad . . .?"

❶ Honest? They check the facts and claims. They want to be absolutely sure their client can back what the ad says.

❷ Believable? The team must be careful because an ad can be honest, but not believable, and vice versa.

❸ Clear? Besides being understandable, the commercial should speak the target audience's language and reflect their attitudes.

❹ Memorable? Memorable doesn't mean shocking or in bad taste. A memorable ad is based on a thought-provoking concept that gives customers a compelling reason to buy a product or service.

❺ And lastly, they want to know: If we replaced our client's logo at the end of the spot with one of our competitors, could they say the same thing we're saying?

It's an effective test because the team can use it to weed out defective spots early, before problems embarrassingly pop up in a presentation, or God forbid, in the middle of production. (It's a fun test, too, and you can experiment with it at home. Just grab a magazine and open it to an ad and ask the five questions. You'll love how many fail the test.)

Allll righty then. Finally, when they have a pile of eight or so commercial ideas that they think are really fantastic, the team presents them to the creative director, who says, "Great. I like these four spots, but fix this and change that." And back they go and buff and polish the spots to the creative director's liking. Then, together, they all go over to present the ideas to the suits, who usually say, "Weellll, this one's okay and that one's off strategy, and we hate that one and we don't get that one at all." And that causes a big argument and the whole process goes through another cycle. In the end, though, when everyone agrees that there are three terrific spots, they get drawn up by a storyboard artist, and the agency troops over to MegaPhone's headquarters to present to the honchos over there.

Welcome to the fun zone. A client presentation is the closest thing to an audition that the creative team ever experiences. This is the moment the agency has to stand up, perform, and *sell*. In fact, a presentation can be the most important, most crucial moment in a client/agency relationship. Anything can happen in one of these meetings and usually does. The MegaFolks could say that the commercials are off strategy or too expensive to produce. Or the agency might flat out do a poor job of presenting the work. A group of people could burst into the middle of the presentation with a birthday cake, singing "Happy Birthday." (Seen it.) The thing is, Mega could mega-dislike the whole dog and pony show and *kill everything*, and the agency would have to go back to square one.

But today, Jenkins & Associates hits a home run. There's a spot that the ten or so MegaPhone people in the room have warm feelings about. It's our brand! It's funny! It's on target! It's within budget! They want to have it produced!

The sperm has hit the egg. Only problem is, the gestation period takes less than a month before this baby appears on the air.

⑤ Preproduction

Did you ever imagine there was so much crap that goes on just to create a commercial? And that's only half of it. We've now arrived at the time period between the day the client approved the ad and the day it shoots. This is called preproduction, or, in ad slang, "pre-pro." Casting is a major part of pre-pro, but before we get into how agencies go about casting, it's valuable to know a couple of things about the mechanics of nailing together a TV commercial before it shoots.

WHO DOES WHAT

After a commercial is approved by the client, a lot of new people get involved with the project. Those that should concern you the most are the agency producer, and, of course, the director.

Agency Producers

Agency producers are amazing people. They not only know the filmmaking process from beginning to end, they're also responsible for controlling the budget. Their primary concern is delivering the job on time and for the money.

But what blows me away is that they're like walking databases of information on directors, production companies, locations, restaurants, phone numbers, casting directors—and actors. Every Los Angeles producer that I've worked with has been familiar with just about every face in town at any given time. They have strong relationships with most casting directors, and most of them know talent when they see it. This (and the fact that talent costs money) gives them a huge say in casting decisions. Experienced agency producers are very savvy—sometimes scarily preternatural—about actors who will, or won't, work in their commercial, and in casting sessions, they can be notoriously swift and brutal when looking at audition tapes. These hardworking people have to act decisively, because once the ignition has been switched on and the production is smokin' its tires, they don't have time for people who waste their time. They want the best person, right now, or get out of the way. (And mind you, during crunch time the creatives are in the same mood.)

Directors

All directors are employed by production companies (some have their own) and, therefore, their reputations are tied to the company. The fact that commercials are a function of advertising means that there are all kinds of commercial directors, each with skills that suit them to a particular commercial genre. As in film, they tend to concentrate on notable skill areas to remain visible and hirable. Some are good at directing comedy, others are great with action, some only shoot car spots, there's a niche that only works in fashion, and some direct kids very well. There are even directors who only shoot food. (Probably because food doesn't talk.) What you should be hoping for is someone who likes to work with people.

Some commercial directors are working toward careers in the motion-picture business. Not surprisingly, there are quite a few film directors who direct commercials. Many get their chops from directing music videos. The late, great Brian Gibson began working for the BBC directing scientific documentaries. Directors come from nonentertainment backgrounds, too, such as still photography or fine art. And make a note of this: some are ex-agency people! So, be aware that whomever you're going to audition for may or *may not* know how to work very well with actors. If you sense that you're in front of a director who doesn't have a lot of experience directing actors, it'll be up to you to make him feel comfortable, to make him feel like you'll be easy to work with.

> **TIP:** *Beware that many commercial directors don't have film-school or acting backgrounds.*

Every director has a style, of course, and you can tell one from another by looking at compilations of all their spots on their individual show reels. (I've provided a list of Web sites in chapter 9 where you can locate directors and view their work.) Understandably, some directors are exceptional, and, therefore, charge higher fees than others. Directors like these work for, or own, the better, more expensive production companies and they can cherry-pick the best spots from high-profile agencies with big-name clients. However, there aren't that many directors who hold this lofty position. If you're lucky, you'll audition for one or two throughout your career, but most of the time you'll be up in front of someone who, at the least, has been chosen for his or her competency with the material. That's not to denigrate directors of this caliber. Not at all. The majority of them are very, very good, and they're the ones that do most of the heavy lifting in the business.

CHOOSING A DIRECTOR

The agency producer's first order of business is to choose a director whose style is best suited to shoot the commercial. This, along with the producer's knowledge of a director's abilities and track record, will be the basis for her recommendations to the art director and copywriter, and, ultimately, the agency brass and the client. The producer will review lots and lots of director's show reels, and, in the process, weed out those whose style or ability doesn't fit, and, at the same time, look closely at the production values of the work to try and judge the cost of the kinds of commercials a director directs. (For instance, a director who mostly shoots on location on 35mm film, who utilizes expensive special effects in postproduction, is somebody who prefers shooting big budget commercials. Depending on the budget and the concept, this person may not or *may be* right for the job.) The producer will also be very curious to know how good the director is with talent and how he treats actors, so she'll query casting directors who've had experience with a particular director.

If the producer is unfamiliar with the way a director works, a few phone calls to people who've worked with him will help the producer get a sense of how this person operates. This is very important because a director's temperament and methodology are going to affect a working atmosphere that throws everybody together in a very intense, sweaty push to make a commercial and achieve greatness in a very short time.

And since casting is so crucial, the producer is going to want to know how the director makes his choices. Clio Hall of Fame writer/creative director and agency principal Howie Cohen has worked with hundreds of directors over the years, and offers this observation on the importance of a producer choosing a director who understands how the concept affects the casting of a commercial:

"We choose a director to take the concept and push it to its outer limits, but *within* the concept. Where (a director) can go wrong is trying to create a different idea. You thought you had an agreement on what we're all trying to accomplish and now all of a sudden this director is way outside the boundaries. . . . trying to push the envelope beyond what the story itself calls for. In other words, (trying to) create some sort of 'stamp' that makes the character or the talent more important than the story. It's almost like the film director who makes you conscious about the camera: 'Look how I'm moving the camera!' as opposed to, 'Wow, what a great story.'

"Everybody's looking for some way to stand out or connect, and really, it starts with the concept. If you have a somewhat risky, irreverent concept that you want to try to have stand out, then you should try to cast it that way. If you have a concept that's safe, uninspired— y'know, a legitimate but not particularly exciting concept—then you're going to end up casting it that way and that's the way the spot is going to wind up. Now, you choose the wrong director, he may take that concept and put some irreverent casting in there. Then you've got agency people in a casting session going, 'Why are we doing this? This person doesn't look like a father of two teenage boys with a loving wife living in the suburbs!' And that director will say, 'Well, that'd be dull.' But, that was the casting on the storyboard. That's when you have what's called a bit of a camel."

After all of this prep-work, the producer puts together a tasty stack of directors' show reels, grabs the creative team, and they all troop down the hall to a conference room, where they sit down, pop in tapes, review the work, and make some choices. They watch a lot of reels. They have a lot of heavy discussions about what they see—all of them based on their vision of fulfilling the concept and the strategy, and much of it based on the technical aspects of filmmaking and a director's ability to make the talent believable. Since these are creative people who keep their egos burbling just under the surface, these discussions can get a little, well, *warm* at times, too, because, really, what they're doing is pretty subjective stuff—kind of like those steamy arguments you have with your friends about directors and filmmaking. ("Yeah, he's good. But he's no *Tarantino!*")

Ultimately, four or five directors are chosen (and approved by the agency top guns) and the producer sends the storyboard to those four or five production companies to see if the director is interested in doing the spot, if he or she is available, and also to have the spot "bid out" (priced). Next, the producer and the creative team interview the interested directors to see whose point of view fits with theirs and who's going to bring fresh thinking to the project.

During the interviews the agency will have the directors explain the way they perceive the concept and have them lay out some ideas they think will make the spot better. Whether this interview is in person or (usually) over the phone, both sides will use the storyboard as a guide to discuss every important element of the commercial, with casting being right up there at the top of the list. They all have definite ideas about the cast—oh my, yes—and a smart agency will ask a lot of questions to make sure a director understands the guidelines, because, as Howie Cohen related, the last thing we want is a war over casting choices in the middle of production. However, when the candidate is ultimately hired as captain of the Spaceship TV Commercial, the creative team and the producer will generally take the director's advice on casting. (I say generally because whether or not the art director or copywriter have any commercial, entertainment, or acting experience, their egos won't prevent them from having a say in casting decisions.)

Since most directors have Type A personalities, there's a comfort-level evaluation that goes back and forth during these meetings, as well. We've got to feel like this is somebody we can hang with for a couple of weeks, or at least tolerate. We want to be sure that, in the end, the commercial will exceed our expectations. On the other hand, the director wants to be comfortable that his oeuvre will be enhanced and his reputation advanced. Personal chemistry is important on both sides.

Finally, when the director with the right stuff says the right things and the money's right, and the client approves, the job is awarded. And pre-pro, which includes casting (at last), begins.

THE CASTING PROCESS

Compared to other casting situations, the short production time frame and the fact that commercials are designed to sell something make a big difference in casting criteria and decision making. The ad agency gets stressed out because casting problems can cause delays and delays cost money. Bottom line, the agency is always focused on what we are trying to sell, and our decisions are based on what the spot is trying to achieve. *How* we do this is a demonstration of all those important DNA elements highlighted earlier.

So, here's what happens: First, a casting director is hired. Sometimes the director will request a favorite casting director because they've enjoyed a successful relationship, sometimes someone will be hired because she specializes in casting certain people, like athletes or models, for instance. Meanwhile, the director and his producer get together with the agency team and talk about the cast. Sometimes the director will have favorite actors, and if there aren't conflicts (someone's been in a competitor's commercial, for example), they'll be called in to read.

Usually, since the creatives have such a deep understanding of the spot, they'll talk with the casting director and give her a lot of input. They'll read them the script with as much emotion as they can, and maybe send over a storyboard and go into great detail as to what the spot's about and how it will look and feel. But more importantly, they spell out how the talent looks, their age, ethnicity, and, specifically, what they do in the spot and who they *are*. This is crucial because it goes right to the psychological gesture of the character, and, therefore, I've always felt it's important to try to give the casting director a potent example of the character's background. The trick, though, is to give the casting director just the right amount of input so she can use her imagination and skills. If we communicate well, and the casting director is really clever, we'll see some interesting people.

Next, the casting director contacts agents for talent (or if it's a non-union spot, rounds up actors they know and like). Once the list of talent is assembled, the casting director holds the initial call taping session. (Note: an initial call is also known as a *pre-read* in the film and TV business. Pre-reads can be a bigger test for actors because the show's producers may be present. Since the producers have the final say in casting their show, they can make hiring decisions on the spot.)

Immediately afterward, tapes of these auditions are sent to the agency team and the director. After they review the auditions, a short list of actors is selected for the callback. At the callback, two or three actors are selected for each part and, shortly thereafter, their taped performances are shown to the client, who—with the agency and director's recommendations—makes the final decision.

And away we go.

TIP: *No matter what anybody thinks, as far as the client is concerned, their product is the star of the commercial, not you.*

⑥ Ordinary People Watch TV for the Entertainment; Commercial Actors Watch TV for the Commercials

Would you like a free education that'll make you a better commercial actor? Of course you would, and there's a teacher standing by ready to start classes immediately. It's your TV set and your VCR or DVD player (or whatever recording technology you use). They're your windows into ad agency thinking.

Now that you've read the "Process" sections of chapter 4, you should have a fair idea of the elements at work inside a commercial—the concept, the brand personality, the tone and manner, and the target market—but now it's time to really take a look at those advertising motivators and make them work for you. So, from now on, you're going to watch commercials with a new point of view—not merely watch them—but study them like ad people do. Why? Because most commercials are a direct expression of the script, and to some extent, the storyboard.★ And both are based on that all-important creative brief, the genesis of all ads.

By doing a little homework a whole new world of acting possibilities will open up for you, so that when you come in to audition and see a script and storyboard for the first time, you'll not only have a better understanding of what's going on with the spot, you'll know how you fit

---

★ *The storyboard is really the first generation of a* shooting board, *which is the detailed, shot by shot, angle by angle guide the director and his team use to map out the shoot. It would be nice if you could see a shooting board at a call, but you never will.*

in. You'll see that the key elements that motivate the spot are the same elements that motivate your choices.

What's more, if you study commercials for awhile, you'll begin to develop an eye for new trends: What's hot, what's going on out there in the world of broadcast advertising, so that someday when an agent or casting director says to you, "This is one of those new Mentos commercials," you won't be in the dark about those hip new Mentos ads. You'll know how to approach the work.

HOW TO GET THE MOST OUT OF STUDYING TV COMMERCIALS

Do this: Watch TV and record a variety of thirty-second commercials that have actors in them who look like your type. Preferably, you'll want TV ads that meet our "set the bar high" criteria for maximum dialogue, maximum character screen-time, and overall high quality. And you'll want to avoid recording spots that are heavy on the product and light on the talent, such as car commercials—they spend most of their thirty seconds with running footage showing off the sheet metal.

Here's how to get started. For example, let's say you're a woman between twenty-five and thirty-five years old, average looking, and quick-witted, you work out at the gym but you're not an athlete, and your USP connotes someone who's authoritative. Okay, for the sake of this demonstration, we'll assume that two of the types of roles you could be called for are "moms" and "career women." Those are pretty broad categories, but to find commercials to study for those types you can narrow your search by thinking of yourself as a target market. For instance, there are tons of ads directed to moms during afternoon soaps, so record a block of those. Or record a couple of hours of the serious Sunday morning news shows like *Meet the Press* and *Face the Nation*. You'll find authoritative advertising going on during that time period. Even when you casually watch your usual TV shows, keep your VCR or DVD recording because you may come across an unusual choice for a type like yours, and you'll want to investigate that as well. Whoever you are, keep your eyes open for the kinds of roles you're most likely to audition for, and replay them over and over so you can watch what the actors do. Get to know those people. Study their performances. Try to get a sense of the variety of characters that they play.

> **TIP**: *Think of yourself as the target market.*

Another terrific resource for studying commercials is the Web. Many major advertisers proudly display their ads on their Web sites, and you can view them over and over to your heart's content. If you've recorded something or seen some advertising on air that meets your criteria, check out that company's site. They may even have an archive of their ads, which can provide you with a rich history of their brand and its DNA. As you'll discover later in this book, a company Web site can give you heaps of inside information that you can use if you happen to be auditioning for one of their commercials.

> **TIP**: *Many advertisers run commercials on their Web sites for you to study.*

Finally—either from your recorded source or a Web site—zero in on a commercial that has a good role you could've been cast for. You're already familiar with the DNA of a commercial. Okay, now's the time to look for these key *advertising motivators* as you replay the ad, and try to determine how they're affecting the ad—and the performer.

Here are the elements to look for:

A good place to begin studying is to try to figure out just what the heck the commercial is about. That's obviously the *concept*, as we previously discussed in depth. You'll find it isn't that difficult to recognize a concept as you run a commercial because 99 percent of the time, it's playing out right there in front of you as a completed piece of work. But when you come in to audition, there are times when the concept doesn't stand out in a script or storyboard. So, the objective is to get familiar with concepts in a relaxed situation at home, so that later on you'll have a better chance of recognizing one in a naked script. Remember that a TV commercial concept will be directly related to the prospect of either selling something or creating a strong bond between the target market and the advertiser. To refresh your memory, here are a couple of real concepts seen on TV while writing this book:

"S------'s television picture is so realistic, you'll feel like you're actually part of the action."

"M--------- orange juice is so fresh, it tastes like it comes directly from the grove."

"People will do anything to get free ----------."

"If you don't quit smoking, you'll only have a *ghost* of a chance to enjoy playing with your grandson."

Get the picture?

After spending some time on the concept, ask yourself, "Who are they selling to?" That's the *target market,* and, as we've discussed, the target's needs and desires will dictate the way the advertiser *talks* to them. (See below.) When casting specs are sent to a casting director, those specs take the target market into consideration, and that's why your type was called. Those specs are 75 percent of the battle. You're going to plug in the rest.

Knowing who the target market is can be crucial, because the realization can help you answer this potent question: "What is my purpose in this commercial?" Mostly, you'll be called for roles that are essentially "you as the target market." But here's the rub: Occasionally you're going to run across a commercial that, on paper at least, doesn't make any sense in its casting. You'll need to know what you're doing in the commercial.

TIP: *Ask yourself, "What is my purpose in this commercial?"*

Here's a case—it's very sad, actually—but it goes a long way to demonstrate the value of asking why you're looking at a part that doesn't seem to fit your type. Recently, a small cellular phone company ran a campaign directed at high school and college-aged kids to sell them a hot new phone. Strangely, the ads featured older men and women—and I mean *really old people*—behaving like teenagers, hanging out around some tricked-out cars, dancing, talking smack. Their behavior was all very incongruous and embarrassing to watch until I asked the question, "What is their purpose in this commercial? Why are these old people acting like this?" And that's when I could smell the problem: This spot was making punks of them because the target kids think it's cool to make fun of old people! "We're not old! Therefore, this new phone is cool!"

If you were looking at that script and thought, "Well, this is weird—I'm an old geezer acting like a kid? Why am I doing this?" Then you might have realized the intent of the commercial: to sell phones to young buyers this company had to be hip and irreverent (which was their brand personality, by the way). In the end, that meant that you were going to be the butt of a joke. This campaign was in such poor taste that it made me wonder why anyone would want to appear in it, especially senior citizens. Obviously, those that did appear didn't spend much time wondering—or asking—about who was supposed to buy the phones and what motivated them. Had they done that, they may have opted out, too.

Question what the person you're watching is doing in the spot. Question every spot. Then, someday you'll look at a script and understand that you might be representing an allegorical concept like "the heart of the city." Or you're here to speak for the millions of kids who think they're being duped by tobacco companies. Or you're here as a straight man to set up a joke at the end of the script. Or you're simply somebody who really likes cranberry juice. And so forth.

Next, see if you can figure out the advertiser's *brand personality*. Who is this company? Are they cool? Snobby? Xtreme? Your next-door neighbor?

Jay Leno? David Letterman? Good brand personalities should have qualities similar to people you know in life. Try to imagine why your personality would (or wouldn't) work with theirs.

TIP: *Look for the advertiser's brand personality.*

One giveaway to a brand's personality is its slogan. For instance, for years, Allstate Insurance has claimed, "You're in good hands." They're the "good hands people." The connotation is that they're warm, protective, and caring. That's their personality and that's what the target market wants to hear.

Granted, you'll find that many advertisers don't use a slogan, but after a couple of replays it shouldn't be too hard to sniff out their personalities, too.

Unfortunately, many advertisers don't know or even care about their brand personalities, and that always results in advertising that's either vague or just plain dumb-ass annoying. You see spots like this on air all the time. Still, it can't hurt to record some of them, too, and imagine what *your* personality, USP, and ability could have done to make them better.

As you continue to scrutinize your commercials, don't lose sight of the fact that what you're watching is a *finished product*. The commercial has been edited, sound effects and music have been added, and special effects have been laid in. Take that into consideration when investigating the following components.

Look at how the spot is *executed*, or carried out. The way a commercial is executed is really the bone structure, skin texture, eye color, body rhythms, gender, heart, and *soul* of the brand personality. For instance, until recently, Allstate spots have featured local insurance agents appearing in down-home environments who spoke reassuringly to the camera. (Sorry, these were real people, not actors.) The spots were shot with warm colors, the camera work was dreamy, and there wasn't a lot of editing going on. The music had an "American" feel to it. All of these elements added up to the *tone* and *manner* of the execution, resulting in the singular expression of the brand personality, which is its most basic *tone of voice*. Voilà! "You're in good hands with Allstate."

But suddenly, Allstate changed their campaign. Now it features a well-known actor who appears in various locales—a courtroom, the side of a highway, each one having something to do with an Allstate benefit—delivering new Allstate sales messages. But the thing is, even though the new Allstate campaign may look different, it's not: The actor is warmly assuring. Everything is shot in soft, muted colors. The music is gentle, and has an "American" feel to it. Most of the camera work consists of one long dolly in on the talent. Sound familiar? Yep, "You're *still* in good hands with Allstate even though we've cosmeticized our commercials."

> **TIP:** *Try to get a feel for the commercial's tone and manner.*

Look at the spot *you've* recorded and try to get a feel for its tone and manner. Listen to the way your commercial talks, verbally and visually. If there are other commercials from the same advertiser, record and compare yours with those. If the same tone and manner appear in those, that's the trait of their entire campaign, as with Allstate. But note that in some campaigns the tone and manner could differ slightly from one ad to another. That's because they may have different subsets to their target market. For instance, a car manufacturer may have a familiar theme that runs throughout all their ads, but the company must talk to their luxury-car buyers in a different manner than their SUV buyers because each group has different needs and desires.

Execution is also a function of how the commercial is constructed and edited (or "cut"). Some may be a linear story with a beginning, middle, and end. Some are odd bits and pieces that all add up to fulfilling the plot. There could be two stories being told at once using an editing style called crosscutting. The voice-over (designated "VO" on scripts) could be saying something entirely different than the action. In any case, observe construction so that, at the very least, you'll know that when a script or storyboard looks slightly out of kilter it's been constructed that way for a reason.

Once you get a feel for how commercials are constructed, isolate one or two and try to visualize each one as a storyboard. The way to do this is to turn off the sound, press play, and just watch the action. That's as close to looking at a storyboard as you can get. As you'll discover in chapter 8, storyboards are laid out in key scenes called "frames," and each frame contains a lot of information. Just like any film or TV show, an ad will be a series of expanded versions of the frames broken out into separate, cohesive shots, each separated by an edit (or other editing techniques such as a dissolve or a soft cut). This silent screening gives you the advantage of focusing on each shot as it relates to the rest. After a few run-throughs, even the most complex piece of filmmaking can start to make sense.

Now here's a very revealing exercise to try: Record an ad with lots of dialogue in it and copy the dialogue down on paper as you would a script. Now replay the spot with the sound off and compare the dialogue with the action. You may discover that the action says one thing and the words say another.

What else will you discover with the sound off? Well golly, there's *no music*. That's a significant element of tone and manner, and when it's missing, we must rely on the drama provided by the film. Same thing at an audition: Unless you're called to sing or dance, there's slight chance that music will be playing, and you'll have to rely on the script and board to create the mood for you. Reading for an advertiser where you've discovered the style of music they use in their ads could be helpful.

Closely related to the way an ad is executed is the question of how the sales message is being conveyed. There comes to mind a recent spot for a line of pickup trucks that told the story of the automaker's new truck in a subtle but memorable way. The concept was that the trucks are built to last for such a long time that fathers hand them down to sons. The entire thirty seconds focused on an ex-rodeo cowboy who's teaching his son how to rope. When the kid succeeded in tossing his lariat, Dad handed him his big old rodeo belt buckle as his reward. Throughout the spot the pickup truck was just unobtrusively *there* in most of the scenes, and a subtle voice-over provided facts about it. Point is: The gesture of giving the belt buckle to the son foreshadowed the day when the son would get that truck for his own. The cowboy and his son personified the long-lasting value of the truck, and their relationship conveyed the message in a very warm way.

This is just one of the many methods ad agencies utilize to convey the sales message and we'll cover them next in "Executional Styles."

Finally, record commercials from other advertisers who compete with the one or ones you've been studying, and compare them. (Soft drinks, lending institutions, and fast-food restaurants are good examples, because these companies crank out a lot of ads and there are always lots to compare.) Although they're in the same categories, you'll begin to appreciate the differences in concept, brand personality, execution, tone and manner, etc., that are the dynamics of each advertiser's effort.

> **TIP:** *Compare your selected spot with the competition.*

Along the way, if you run across a talent who works a lot, try to record his or her performances, too. If you can get a few examples of this person in different commercials, so much the better. And it doesn't really make much difference if that person is your type, either, because what you want to ascertain is, "What is it about that actor that makes him get cast in all these commercials? What's *his* USP?" You may be inspired to think about your special quality as it relates to the material you're studying.

Once you develop a mind-set for looking at TV spots with this new ad agency perspective, you should be able to come up with some fairly accurate observations that you can eventually apply when a script is handed to you. Ultimately, you'll be better prepared to answer: "How does this commercial affect me? How do I behave in this commercial?"

EXECUTIONAL STYLES

When the creative team is brainstorming ideas, they'll also incorporate an executional style that works best to build a creative skeleton for the ad.

> **TIP:** *Every commercial you read for will have a method of conveying the sales message.*

These executional styles, or more appropriately, the various methods of executing the sales message, are very familiar to most people, even if they aren't acutely aware of them when they see 'em. Let's investigate these methods for a moment, so later on when you're studying your recorded commercials, you can keep them in mind and see if you can identify which one the ad agency has built its ad around. In all cases, the style will have a general influence on how your character behaves in the ad. But in a few cases, the style can create important transitions within a commercial that can cause you to make decisions about the way you play it.

Before we begin, I'd like to mention that there are a couple of good acting books out there that attempt to categorize these styles and then offer advice as to how you should act in them. You may want to check these out, but as far as I'm concerned, there are just too many variables in commercials, and I think that trying to adopt a particular line of attack in acting for a particular style is just beating your head against the wall. There isn't any "one size fits all" approach to acting in commercials. Just be true to the work and strive towards being better at *being*.

All right? Ahem, let's proceed.

The most common style is the *Problem/Solution* commercial. Typically—and you've seen this a million times—the advertiser's product or service comes to the rescue in some winning fashion by removing an ugly stain or enhancing a dull meal. These ads blatantly highlight the product's USP.

Closely related to Problem/Solution spots are *Product Demonstration* ads, in which the product not only comes to the rescue, but you get to see how the darn thing works doing it! Sometimes products need to be demonstrated because we wouldn't believe they actually work unless we see it with our own eyes—and often they can actually be very informative. The downside of product demo ads is that so many of them rely on stupid, over-the-top scenarios. You can just imagine a creative team sitting in their office in full brainstorm going, "Okay these people have heartburn, acid indigestion, right? So their insides are literally *on fire*! Smoke comes out of their . . ." Puh-leeze.

Next are *Testimonials*. Sometimes you'll see these with actual real-life people in them touting the benefits of their new weight-loss program (or what have you) but mostly it's real-life actors who appear in these spots. The concepts are the same: Talk up the product benefits while making us believe that all this praise comes from a personal opinion or experience. (Celebrity endorsements are Testimonials, too, but you won't have to worry about them until you become famous.) These kinds of spots are particularly good for actors because of the challenge of making their performances really believable. I once worked on a long-running fast-food campaign where most of the ads consisted of a monologue from a real-life character sitting in familiar surroundings just talking real-life stuff about the food. Interesting to note that most talent found it tough to make those monologues believable in a cold read. Ad-copy monologues are something you really need to concentrate on in class.

Akin to Testimonials are *Spokesperson* ads. A Spokesperson is similar to someone in a Testimonial in that they're endorsing a product or service, but a spokesperson is more likely to be overtly *pitching* the product instead of just talking about it like a normal human being. Therefore, the ad copy is more than likely a straight sell that comes with a laundry list of product benefits and even sale prices. Another difference between a Spokesperson and a Testimonial is that the actual spokesperson (or sometimes the "spokes *it*," since we see a lot of puppets and computerized characters hawking products) is the true representative of the company—the perfect match of personality and product. Ad people sometimes say a spokesperson puts a "face" on the company, and that's why you've seen so many famous faces in them over the years. (Often the spokesperson is the company's CEO up there beating a drum for his product. This is because his ego won't allow anybody else to talk about his precious product, and, except for some rare personalities, these people mostly suck.) But that doesn't mean there aren't spokesperson roles for regular actors like you. Opportunities pop up all the time.

As an actor, being a spokesperson offers a nice challenge because it opposes one of my basic tenets: *Don't Sell!* Actors who can deliver "selly" ad copy without selling are number one in my book, but nonetheless, you may read for a spokesperson and be directed to sell. In that case, close your eyes and take the money. Being a spokesperson can be a long-running and lucrative gig.

Next are the types of commercials I call *Representational* or *Allegorical* because they'll use a character or a situation or some kind of icon to stand for, or personify, a product's attribute or quality. (Remember the rodeo cowboy and his son?) Let's say, for instance, that a company claims that their batteries last longer than others. In one famous campaign, this concept of longevity was represented by an unstoppable windup bunny rabbit. That was achieved with a toy model and computer animation, of course, but you may find yourself looking at a script where your character or your action is meant to represent a concept like "on-time delivery," or "legendary performance," or "a locked-in rate," and then you'll have some interesting choices to make.

An offshoot of a representational style is something I call the *Literal Translation.* These come directly from clichés or familiar expressions like "blow your socks off," or, "she has an ear for music," or, "Dad's a real bear in the morning." Do you see where this is going? Of course you do. The character you read for will literally *have an ear for music*! Somewhere in the spot someone's going to actually have their socks blown off. Dad will grow fur. Be prepared.

One of the most popular ways of executing a concept is the use of *Vignettes.* Webster's defines a vignette as "a brief incident or scene (as in a play or movie)" and these little snippets of action or dialogue allow the commercial-makers the opportunity to pack a lot of scenes and characters into twenty-nine-and-one-half seconds (or less). There are all kinds of vignettes. Sometimes three or four unrelated characters will appear in three or four different scenes, each talking about the same product, but each in a unique way. Or you've probably seen a spot like this: There's one long block of copy in the ad, but instead of one actor performing it, they shoot *eight* actors performing it in eight different locations. Then they take a piece of each actor's performance and edit the whole thing together back into that one block of copy. The result is an interesting variety of performances coming together to tell a story.

Vignettes can appear disjointed if taken apart. Little slices of life, small telling pieces of action, or one or two important words taken on their own don't mean anything, but together, they can add up to a powerful statement. Vignettes are a good vehicle for flashbacks, too, and if you encounter a scene that appears to be a flashback and you're uncertain, for certain, *ask* about it.

Another style is *What If?* In these spots, the characters are usually trying to come up with a solution to a dilemma of some kind, and one of them will say something like, "Gee, what if we tried strapping a jet power pack on the deliveryman's back!" Ripple dissolve to the What If? dream sequence where the deliveryman jets off skyward and flies crazily into the side of a building. Generally, the What If? solution fails miserably in these ads, proving that the old tried-and-true way this advertiser does business is the best way. Sometimes, however, the What If? outcome is successful, demonstrating the advertiser's ingenuity and facility at coming up with ideas making life better for all of us. Once again, actors need to be careful to understand whether the What If? part is genuine or facetious.

The style that most people seem to identify with the most are *Real-Life* (sometimes called *Slice-of-Life*) commercials, and since they tackle all kinds of products and situations, Real-Life is really more of a catchall category. There can be Real-Life Problem/Solution ads, Real-Life Testimonials, and Real-Life Vignettes. In any case they all attempt to portray a slice of life in a way that's familiar and similar to the target market's zone of reality.

Now, turn up the heat on Real-Life and you've got *Extreme Reality*. These ads can range from scenarios that stretch our ideas of what's familiar, all the way over to concepts so out there that they make something unbelievable, believable. To illustrate, at this writing, there is a soft drink that's corralled the "Xtreme" lifestyle for males in their teens and twenties. All the guys in the commercials look, talk, and act like they belong on a snowboard or a motocross bike, but everything real that happens to them is pumped up. (The guy doesn't just jump a bike over any old canyon, it's the *Grand* Canyon. In one spot, a hiker butts heads with a bighorn ram.) The reason these spots are so popular with these young guys is that the cola advertiser has captured *their* reality—juiced-up, in-your-face fun. That's a very significant distinction, because once again we come around to the importance of how the target market views life and what motivates them. As an actor, it'll be up to you to plug yourself into the "real-life" of a particular target-market situation—whatever that may be—and make yourself believable.

One step up from Extreme Reality is *Fantasy*. This is the world of talking animals and people walking on your teeth holding giant toothbrushes. Computer Generated Imaging (CGI) is a popular tool because *it can make anything happen.* But no matter what happens in a Fantasy-based spot, your character will have the same responsibilities as in any other style of commercial.

Over the past few years, some alternative-minded advertisers have been airing a new style of TV commercial that's like Real-Life or even Extreme Reality, but then again, it isn't. Some people call this, what else, "alternative advertising," and rightly so, because these ads go against the grain of traditional advertising in that they don't seem to be trying to actually sell something. They intentionally avoid advertising clichés. Their goal is to be cheesy, campy, and purposely stupid, and I call this style of advertising *Anti-Ads* because it's trying to twist our old notions of what advertising is all about and bend our way of embracing brands in new ways. These ads are all about *brand recognition*. (Brand recognition ads are usually designed to wave at you and go, "Hiii. It's meee. Remember me? Forget about what we're selling. Just remember my name. Buh bye.") Some of this stuff really works, and some of it is dreadful and silly, but I applaud the work because it's fresh and it's setting advertising on its ear. A good way to identify one of these spots is by its compassion for pop culture. As an actor, you may become bewildered while looking for a concept in an Anti-Ad and that's okay. The concept may be too weird to understand. The target market is your best clue. Just be real and flow with it, is all I can say.

Are there other executional styles? Sure, in the Milky Way of advertising new styles are occasionally discovered. But these are the most common, and the most useful for our purposes here. As you can see, each one serves as a shell that holds the inner mechanism of a commercial's DNA. (Wow, two allegories in one sentence!) Those mechanisms are the subject of the next chapter, where we'll begin by providing some eye-opening information about script notations, proceed to a discussion of some common story devices, and, finally, actually tear into some scripts.

But first, it's necessary for us to have a little "heart-to-heart."

DON'T BE A TOMATO

If you've ever seen *Tootsie*, there's a very funny, yet telling, scene where struggling actor Michael Dorsey (Dustin Hoffman) confronts his agent George Fields (Sydney Pollack) about his nowhere career. He's desperate. He asks George to send him up for anything—he doesn't care what it is. George says he can't send him out for *anything* because nobody will hire him. He reminds Michael that he can't even send him out on commercials anymore because on his last gig—where he played a tomato—the shoot went a half day over schedule because *he wouldn't sit down.* "Yes," Michael says in defense, because, "It wasn't logical." "You were a tomato!" his agent yells back. "A tomato doesn't have logic! Tomatoes can't move!" Michael argues that his agent is proving his point, because *if a tomato can't move, how's he going to sit down?*

Do you know obsessive actors like Michael? Are you one? Do you take it too far?

Look, you've just been given a lot of valuable information about advertising—tone and manner, target market, executional styles, and so on—and how it applies to commercials. There's a lot more to come over the next two chapters. So, don't go overboard, okay? Don't be a Michael Dorsey. With so much to absorb, it's easy to overload your head to the point of, well, brain lock. Pick and choose. Take this stuff, cozy up to it to the point where you can make some educated decisions, and then move forward.

TIP: *A little knowledge can go a long way. A lot can be constipating.*

7 Land Mines and Gold Mines in Commercial Scripts

A house doesn't have to fall on you for you to realize by now that all this attention directed at a commercial's DNA—the concept, target market, brand personality, tone and manner, and executional styles (those advertising motivators) are elements you should be aware of when you look at a script for the first time. I hope that you devote time to recording and investigating commercials, so that every time you put your ass on the line for a job, you'll be able to give yourself the advantage that comes with a better understanding of broadcast advertising, and particularly the spot you're reading for.

Look, we both know that most of the time when you pick up a script—any kind of script—most of what you need to know is right there in front of you. But commercials are much more, um, Kafkaesque, and I can't tell you how many times an actor will head off in the wrong direction because he or she failed to understand "What am I doing in this commercial?" or misunderstood the concept, or failed to recognize the brand personality and tone and manner, or were confused about execution or an executional style. So the recommendation here is that if you're at least *familiar* with these elements you'll be buying yourself some cheap audition insurance.

There are additional devices—land mines, or gold mines (it depends on how you deal with them)—that are imbedded in scripts, as well, so let's take a look at them now. Farther along in this chapter we'll run a diagnostic on a couple of scripts to see what makes them tick. Then in the next chapter, we'll pull this all together by scrutinizing two storyboards.

THE FIRST THING TO LOOK FOR IN A SCRIPT

Some of you more experienced people who are reading this are going to say, "I know pretty much what to look for in a script, okay?" But I'll bet there's something some of you always miss. Take a look at our Rita's Fajitas script from the ad agency printed below. Look hard.

TELEVISION

GENERATOR

DATE: 2/23/04 R. 1	COM. #: RFT 1420 :30 SECS.
CLIENT: RITA'S FAJITAS	AIR DATE: 3/3/04
PRODUCT: SPICY FAJITA WRAP	TITLE: JAZZ GUY
JOB #: RF 4704TV	DESCRIPTION: TEST S.F./SLC/LA

CR DIR: JDW   ART DIR: MM COPY: ASM ACCT EX: TR ACCT SUP: DW
CLIENT: D. Schumacher   TRAFFIC: RB

Video	*Audio*
INT NIGHT CLUB	MUSIC
	JAZZ MUSICIAN: This Rita's Fajita Wrap is really cool. Well really it's hot 'cause it's spicy and that's what makes it so cool. Not spicy spicy 'cause that's too hot, but spicy just right, and that's so cool, it's *hot*. Isn't that right? (HE TAKES A BITE OF THE WRAP.)
CLOSE UP PRODUCT	ANNCR VO: Here's how to eat chicken. With some spice to it. The Spicy Fajita Wrap, at Rita's.
SUPER: Spicy Fajita Wrap	
RITA'S LOGO	JAZZ MUSICIAN: It's too cool for this room.

What is it? It's the *date*. Up there. On the top of the script. See it? That's the date the script was approved. Always make a note of it at the initial call because if you're lucky enough to get a callback, you definitely want to check if that date has changed *because that means the script has changed*! If changes have been made to the script, then you may have to make adjustments to your performance.

Sometimes the notation "R1" or "R2" will appear next to the date. That's a big clue as well, because it connotes the number of times the script has been *Revised*. It could also say "revision 1", but no matter, you need to make a note of it at the initial call and double-check it if you come back later to read at the callback.

> **TIP:** *Look for the approval date at the top of the script. That date—or its revision number—is your clue to a change in the commercial.*

INSTRUCTIONS

Commercial scripts are peppered with video instructions and stage directions. When Shakespeare used stage directions, like these from various scenes in *Hamlet*, he meant it:

[*Takes the skull*

[*Makes a pass through the arras*

[*King dies*

[*Dies*

Same with TV commercials. You'll see video instructions like this:

OPEN ON MEDIEVAL-CASTLE COURTYARD

Camera instructions look like this:

CAMERA PULLS BACK TO REVEAL BOOM BOX

And stage directions look like these:

She takes a sip of Coke.

He bites into the burger.

Within a script, these brief, blatant instructions may be called out on the video side of the page and the audio side, or if the script format is stacked they might be given space above and below. Sometimes a script will highlight video instructions by CAPITALIZING them and sometimes not. Stage directions may be *italicized*, or may not.

A storyboard may highlight these notations inside a window placed below or next to the drawn frame, or there may be something happening inside the frame to reflect the action. For instance, you may see an arrow drawn to indicate a camera move. Or you could see a character's expression change from benign to happy to delirious all in one frame. Later on in the chapter about storyboards you'll have an opportunity to see a few demonstrations of these instructions at work.

Obviously you don't want to fail to miss these guideposts, because in some cases they can be just as important as a key piece of sales copy. Usually they help show off a product attribute—like "the clean crisp taste of mountain spring water"—but, just like any other kind of script, stage instructions can hip you to important moments in the action. If you saw the instructions *He takes a sip*, that phrase would surely lead you to make a different acting choice than if you saw *He knocks it back*. Acting 101, right? Still, actors sometimes miss these in auditions and end up looking foolish.

Familiar dramatic instructions appear in scripts as well (*He's surprised, Doris confides in her daughter*). But since this is the wild, weird, anything-goes world of broadcast advertising beware of misinterpreting what you see on the page. What if you looked at a script and you read the colorful phrase *She has a bug up her butt*? That could mean she's perturbed about the situation, or, because this is a TV commercial, *she really does have a bug up her butt*!

Later on, this book will address the degree of questions you can ask at a casting session, but you can file this one away: If an instruction appears to possess several different meanings, ask for clarification.

> **TIP:** *If an instruction appears to have a double meaning, it's okay to ask for clarification.*

Scripts and boards are also littered with abbreviations and shorthand that are part of the language of filmmaking and storytelling. You've probably seen or heard a lot of this stuff before, but it's still good to know these common notations in case you bump up against one and don't know if it's important or not. Here's a list of film terms you're likely to encounter. These first few are the ones requiring the most attention.

> **TIP:** *Know your filmmaking shorthand.*

VO stands for Voice-Over. This is the recording of a person talking that's laid over the picture. Often you'll see ANNCR VO for the announcer. Sometimes it'll be a character, such as DETECTIVE VO. Always pay attention to what's written for the VO.

OC doesn't mean Orange County. It stands for Off Camera. Your character could be talking OC. A baby could be crying OC.

SFX and FX usually stand for Sound Effects, or Effects or Special Effects, and you'll see something like SFX: SQUEALING TIRES, or FX: GLOWING SNOWBALL. Sometimes writers use SFX to indicate music. In any case, the effect will be spelled out after the abbreviation, and you should determine if it has something to do with your action.

SUPER (sometimes called a CARD or TITLE). You've already been alerted to these words or graphics that appear on the screen. More show up in the storyboard chapter.

EXT and INT are abbreviations for Exterior and Interior and inform you whether you're inside or outside.

MOS means filming without sound. MOS comes from the early days of cinema when German filmmakers would say, "All right, ve are shooting mit out sound." (Honest.)

MUSIC. Yep, this would be where the music goes.

POV is Point of View. Not an opinion, but the place from where the camera is looking. If I'm sitting across the room looking at you, that's my POV. (Just like this book.)

The terms in this next category are all *framing* descriptions, which specify how near or far the camera is from a subject. It's a common way to illustrate a shot, and, occasionally, a shot's framing will cause you to alter your behavior at a casting session.

If you'd like to experiment with framing right now, take your two hands and form a window with your thumbs and index fingers opposing each other. Now watch as you move this box in and out from an object. That's basic framing. Most framing names are self-descriptive.

ECU stands for Extreme Close-up.

CU stands for Close-up (As in, "I'm ready for my close-up, Mr. DeMille.") Sometimes the word "Tight" is used, as in TIGHT CU.

MCU, or Medium CU, is a Medium Close-up.

WIDE is, umm, a wide shot.

There are all sorts of camera moves that are achieved by either moving the camera, or a part of the camera, or utilizing the lens. These are:

A PAN is where the camera sweeps over to, or across, the subject from a fixed location. A pan can also be achieved with a DOLLY, which is accomplished by moving the camera itself past the subject. A dolly can also be used to TRACK a moving subject, follow something or someone, or move in or away. Sometimes these moves are called a PUSH IN or PUSH OUT. ZOOMS use the lens in a variety of ways to push in or out. TILTS are up or down pans.

CUT TO, DISSOLVE, WIPE, FADE UP, and FADE OUT are editing techniques used to transition from one scene or one shot to another. They're called "edits." The techniques they describe aren't as important as the fact that edits tell you when a scene ends and begins.

You might see a lot of edits in a script, which means there are many shots, and, therefore it is a fast-paced commercial, or maybe a Vignette. Conversely, fewer edits could mean a slower pace.

> **TIP:** *Filmmaking instructions are road signs guiding you through a script.*

Instructions are great because they add structure to the script, move dramatic traffic, and often tell you what you're doing. They're overt. The next few sections offer a sampling of familiar *devices* used in everything from sitcoms to TV commercials. Some are overt. Some of these like to hide inside scripts.

PUNCH LINES

DOCTOR: I've got good news and bad news. First the bad. You've got two months to live.

PATIENT: (Gulp) What's the good news?

DOCTOR: I just saved a bundle on my car insurance with InsuraCo.

Oh my. This old chestnut of a joke (with the punch line cleaned up and turned into a product endorsement) was actually used as the basis for a recent commercial in a loan company's campaign. It's here to illustrate that, no matter how lame the joke, it still needs to be treated with the reverence any comic piece deserves. As you know, the cardinal rule of comedy is "keep it real" and that's what makes a joke or a story funny. The more real, the more believable.

I'm not saying that everything you read is going to be, or needs to be hilarious, but here's a piece of advice. If you handle a joke well, never mind making the target market laugh when the commercial airs. What's more important is what's happening in the casting session *right now*. If you can get the agency copywriter (who's probably a frustrated screenwriter) sitting back there in the dark to at least *smile* at the joke he's slaved over, then you've just increased your chances of getting hired.

PUNS

"Two boll weevils grew up in South Carolina. One went to Hollywood and became a famous actor. The other stayed behind in the cotton fields and never amounted to much. Naturally, he became known as the lesser of two weevils."

Ever since the dawn of advertising, even before the Egyptians began using hieroglyphics with subliminal messages, puns have been used as a creative staple. Puns are everywhere in advertising, mostly because they're such an easy, low-rent way of conveying an idea. Some commercials have puns in them. Some ads are *built* on puns, but I wouldn't really call them an executional style. Some will take a song and twist it with a pun, like the country classic "Stand by your bran." (Lord help us!) In any case, you shouldn't have any trouble identifying one. (I hope.)

REVEALS

A *reveal* is a device that works with most executional styles. You're already familiar with the way they operate: A secret is disclosed in some clever way, usually by making you think that one thing is happening when it really isn't. You see this device used in sitcoms all the time—Ted is talking about a woman who you think is his wife, but it's revealed that it's actually his sister. Cue the laughter. And, of course, even Shakespeare loved it. (Mistaken twins sound familiar?) Pretense can be fun because it involves a surprise disclosure. As an actor, you need to take a close look at the script, because it won't be much fun for you during the audition if you haven't realized that your spot uses a reveal.

IS THERE A SURPRISE IN THERE?

You've probably read for, or played a part where the script was saying one thing, but you were really playing against it. This dichotomy, this opposition of word and action, can lead to some really interesting drama or comedy, and it often appears in commercials, usually as a reveal.

For instance, there's a commercial running these days that features a nice guy in his late thirties who's pictured in scene after scene enjoying the trappings of a really nice lifestyle. Each time we see him, he proudly gushes about his new car, his country-club membership, his kids who are in good schools, and so on. In the end, he asks rhetorically, "How do I do it? I'm in debt up to my eyeballs." And then he delivers the killer line: "Somebody help me." Now, if you looked at that naked script, you could surmise that this character is a guy who's in way over his head, and you could choose to play him as a rather desperate fellow. That last line could be delivered as a real cry for help: "Somebody *help* me!!" Au contraire, my friend, because the deliciousness of that spot, the thing that made it so funny, was how *opposite* the actor played it. He acted as if he was almost blissfully stunned by his situation, and in the end, his request for help was almost *polite*. Totally opposite to the expected, and totally memorable. He found the nice surprise.

ALL THAT JAZZ

Surprises can also come in the form of an idiom that's indigenous to a character or a culture. You not only have to find those gems, how you

INTERIOR NIGHT CLUB

MUSIC

JAZZ MUSICIAN:

> This Rita's Fajita Wrap is really cool. Well
>
> really it's hot 'cause it's spicy and that's what makes it so
>
> cool. Not spicy spicy 'cause that's too hot, but spicy just
>
> right, and that's so cool it's hot. Isn't that right?
>
> (He takes a bite.)

ANNCR VO:

> Here's how to eat chicken. With some spice to it.
>
> The Spicy Fajita Wrap. At Rita's.

JAZZ MUSICIAN:

> It's too cool for this room.

handle them could make or break your chances of moving forward. Take a few minutes to ingest the script for Rita's Fajitas, reprinted below, and see if you can find the jazz musician's word or expression that adds to the authenticity of the spot. Finding it may be easy. How you'd play it may not.

Did you find it? Okay, hang on to that thought for a second. Before we get to it, let's talk about this commercial first. Let's analyze it.

Unlike some subsequent scripts (and storyboards), we're going to analyze this one without any background information. But even at face value, this script will divulge a lot of useful stuff.

To begin with, how would we categorize this ad in regard to its executional style? Obviously it's a Testimonial monologue with a (slightly pushed) air of Real-Life to it: Here we have a jazz player (Bass? Sax? Keyboard? Don't know.) holding a fajita wrap and talking rather poetically about it. Apparently this thing is spicy 'cause the word *spicy* appears six times.

The fact that we have a jazz musician sitting in a nightclub (says so in the video instructions) talking in a sort of jazz patois is a pretty good indication that the *tone* and *manner* of this spot is pretty laid back. It's not a long script, either. It feels like there's room to breathe. Plus, even though there isn't a storyboard to refer to, there aren't but three scene changes indicated in the video instructions, so we can assume there aren't many edits, contributing to a languid feel. The spot isn't tarted up with SFX or anything else to make it more memorable—the musician is simply talking to us.

Guessing that these could be the attributes of previous ads in Rita's campaign, we could suppose that Rita's *brand personality* is akin to a good friend—probably a colorful personality, as well—who'd sit down and chat with you. So, taking all of this into consideration, you probably wouldn't choose to play the jazz musician as someone with a hopped-up personality.

Now here's one for you: Why is a jazz musician a good choice to sell this product? Why not a hip-hop artist or a salsa singer? They'd be good choices because it's likely that they'd eat something spicy like this sandwich, but the agency used a jazz musician because—for a mainstream target market—he's somebody who'd really know the difference between cool and hot. In fact, that's the signpost to the *concept* of this commercial: Only somebody who knows what's cool and what's hot (a jazz musician) can really describe the interesting harmony of flavors in this fajita wrap. (Inside info: the creative brief specifically said that the commercial had to play up the "spicy, but not overly spicy aspect of the product.") Our jazz guy is also a more universal stereotype than a hip-hop artist or salsa singer so he appeals to a broader target market. Now, when you look at the way the copy is written, you can see why the message about this product comes through in a monologue that almost has a jazz-like riff to it. If you ever met a jazz musician, you might expect him to talk this way.

It's interesting to note that since this product is a *wrap*, the agency could've had a rap artist *rap* about it. That would be a perfect example of a commercial built on a pun: wrap, rap. However, the creative team probably nixed this concept right away because they not only had the good taste to not stoop to doing a spot that relied on a pun, but they'd also seen enough rappers in commercials rhyming for stuff like aluminum foil wrap, Saran Wrap, and Christmas wrapping paper that they felt if they saw another one, let alone had something to do with it, they'd puke.

Okay, did you find the word or expression? If you landed on "It's too cool for this room," you'd be wrong. The key phrase is "Isn't that right?" Here's why:

This script is a version of a commercial that was actually produced. (The names have been changed to protect the innocent.) All along, those three little words at the end of the monologue were the keystone to adding a layer of authenticity to the jazz guy, and they were used as a yardstick during casting.

At the callback it all came down to two really great prospects running neck and neck for the part. Actor number one treated the line like a straight question, and no amount of subtle hinting from the director could get him away from asking "Isn't that right?" as if he were trying to clarify the answer to a math problem. But actor number two understood how the line fit into the overall way the commercial played. He said it like a jazz guy would, not as a question, but as an all-knowing, ironic punctuation. "Isn't that riigghht," he growled. He'd looked at the spot as a whole. He got the part.

ANALYZE THESE

For every executional style there are hundreds of different concepts and a hundred different ways to create a commercial for each concept, so there's no way to include every example for us to look at here. But, just like the Rita's ad, almost every commercial shares the same core elements. By investigating a few more scripts, you ought to do okay with just about anything that comes along.

Take some time to read this script for an allergy medicine called AllerGood. (By the way, just as you'll find at many, many auditions, there isn't a storyboard for this commercial.)

ALLERGOOD
:30 TV

OPEN ON TOUGH LOOKING BIKER
BIKER: I'm afraid of soft fuzzy kittens.

CUT TO LOVEABLE GRANNY
GRANNY: I can't stand flowers.

CUT TO VERY OFFICIOUS-LOOKING WOMAN WITH A LEASH
OFFICIOUS WOMAN: Dogs give me a pain.

CUT TO STONER GUY
STONER GUY: I hate grass bro'.

DISSOLVE TO SHOTS OF: BIKER WITH TEARS RUNNING DOWN
HIS FACE. GRANNY WIELDING MEAN-LOOKING GARDEN SHEARS.
STONER PUTTING ON GAS MASK.

VO: (DURING PREVIOUS SHOTS): If you're like any of these people, you either have some extremely serious personal issues, or you're one of the fifty million Americans who suffer from allergies.

CUT TO OFFICIOUS WOMAN USING ALLERGOOD SQUEEZE BOTTLE.
VO: But now there's 24-hour AllerGood.

CUT TO SHOTS OF: OFFICIOUS WOMAN PRANCING WITH FROU FROU DOG AT DOG SHOW. PROUD GRANNY NEXT TO IMPOSSIBLY LARGE FLOWER ARRANGEMENT. STONER GUY STANDING ON ONE LEG ON RIDING LAWNMOWER DRIVING BY.

VO: (DURING PREVIOUS SHOTS): One squirt of AllerGood and you're good for 24 beautiful hours. AllerGood, and allergies are gone.

CUT TO BIKER HAPPILY FROLICKING WITH A PASSLE OF KITTENS.

Okay, what's one of the first things you noticed about this spot? Obviously, it's a Problem/Solution commercial because we observe that immediately after one of the suffering characters squirts AllerGood up her schnozz, life suddenly becomes beautiful. But that's not as important as the other executional style at work here as well.

Look at the big picture: There are four characters in this script, each appearing alone in *twelve* different scenes. They don't talk to each other, but what they all say and do individually in all these little scenes ultimately adds up to the sales message that "you get twenty-four-hour relief with AllerGood." So, the way this spot is constructed tells us that it's using vignettes to execute the story. Even though your character may be isolated in a vignette, you must pay attention to what the other characters are doing.

Check this: The first four scenes don't tell you anything about the place where your character exists. Later on the script gets more specific about dog shows and lawnmowers—that's apparent—but there's no storyboard, so what do you do? Go ahead and ask, "Where does my opening scene take place?" That would be an okay thing to do, but at an initial call you'll be lucky to have a casting director there to impart this information, so you may have to wing it. At a callback you'll have a better opportunity to find out either from the casting director (who *will* be there) or from the director once you get into the studio.

Now, what about the concept? On the surface, this is not a high-concept commercial—but that's okay, actually, because you'll encounter many scripts where the concept is rather benign. It appears that the theme for this commercial is: "Using AllerGood can really change your life," which is true, but not very funny. What really makes this spot potentially funny and memorable is the familiar device that has people saying one thing when they actually mean something else. So the deeper concept is: "These people aren't what they appear to be." This spot relies on the device of *misdirection*. And the best way to play misdirection is with honest conviction.

Who are these people? They're the target market. Who's the target market? Any adult who suffers from allergies, for sure, but what's arresting here are the types of characters chosen to represent the target market. They're all a bit *odd*. This could be because the advertiser wants to emphasize a wide range of people who'd use the product, but it has more to do with making the spot work better by utilizing what I call "opposites attract" casting. In a case like this, where people say one thing but mean another, it really helps bolster the misdirection concept by featuring characters like, well, heck, we've got a fraidy cat biker, an angry grandma, a straight-laced dog woman, and a stoner guy who doesn't like grass. Just your normal folks here in Mayberry.

What about this brand's personality? Let's pretend for a moment that you received scant information about AllerGood when you received your phone call to come and audition. Even after poking around you couldn't turn up much background data or any previous commercials. Maybe this is AllerGood's very first broadcast effort, which would mean a brand personality hasn't been strongly established. Aha! Now you finally see this script and it confirms that this is AllerGood's maiden run because the VO says, "But *now* there's AllerGood . . ." strongly indicating that it is indeed a new product. That's hardly much to go on, but there *are clues* to the brand personality and the tone and manner of the spot. First of all, the oddball nature of the cast and their behavior is a pretty good indication that AllerGood is comfortable enough not to take itself—and the type of medicine that it sells—too seriously. Even the VO deadpans, "If you're like any of these people, you either have some extremely serious personal issues . . ." So I'd say that the brand personality of the company that makes AllerGood isn't, excuse me, very stuffy. The tone and manner are fun and quirky and slightly edgy. This is the world you'd be living in.

(If a director took this spot and pushed it too far, if he made it tooo wacky, I'd be disappointed because the key to making this thing slyly funny is to play it straight.)

All of which finally leads us to the question, "What is my purpose in this commercial? Why am I acting like this?" I think you'll agree that this is a pretty straightforward commercial. And even though the concept relies on misdirection, the answer to what you're doing in this spot is simply: I'm here to demonstrate the positive benefit of AllerGood. I'm a biker who's allergic to kittens. I'm a gardener who's allergic to flowers. I'm a dog lover who's allergic to dogs. I'm eccentric looking, but in reality, a straight guy (you caught that, didn't you?), who's allergic to mowed lawns.

By the way, this spot appears to run long, doesn't it? There's a lot going on with twelve scenes and whatnot. There's a lot of business on the page. But the beauty of vignettes is that they allow agencies to pack those twenty-nine-point-five seconds with a ton of information. Nonetheless, even though each of these scenes is seemingly compact, you don't want to let the length of a scene influence your performance when you read. Especially in a case like this, don't worry about the time; *don't rush.* Read to get the part, and if you get it, the time issue will be addressed when you shoot, and later if necessary, when the commercial is edited during post-production.

> **TIP :** *When scenes look short, that doesn't mean that when you read, you must rush to do them in the allotted time.*

Before we go on to take a look at storyboards, let's take a brief, loving look at one last commercial.

Dreamy Cream makes ice-cream sandwiches and other kinds of novelties that you'd buy from the ice-cream truck that plays that insane jingle while cruising your neighborhood during the summer, but you can buy their stuff in the grocery store. This ad is for their nut-covered ice-cream cone.

A PHOTOGRAPHER IS SHOOTING A FASHION MODEL
AT A STUDIO.
PHOTOGRAPHER: Good. Hold that.
INNER VOICE: Super model, huh?
PHOTOGRAPHER (To the Inner Voice): Y'know, I just
got rid of that song you put in my head.
INNER VOICE: Ohh. *I* wouldn't do *that*.
PHOTOGRAPHER: Right. (To the model): Now give me
pouty. Give me pouty.
INNER VOICE: Listen to this: Dreamy Cream Fudge
Cone. Chunky chunks of fudge...
PHOTOGRAPHER: Chunky fudge? Give me chunky.
That's it. Give me chunky!
INNER VOICE: Crunchy peanuts.
PHOTOGRAPHER (FIRING AWAY NOW): Nuts! Give me
nuts!
THE MODEL HUFFS OFF.
CUT TO SHOT OF ICE CREAM CONE.
VOICE OVER: Satisfy your inner craving. The Dreamy
Cream Fudge Cone.
CUT TO PHOTOGRAPHER EATING CONE.
INNER VOICE: Got a song for you. (Dreamy Cream jingle
plays: "You'll melt before we do...")

Man, this is one wild little spot. If you were reading for the Photographer, you'd have a lot to contend with: Taking pictures while instructing the Model, going in and out of a conversation with your Inner Voice and finally, flipping out over the fudge and nuts (which is the Dreamy Cream USP).

By the way, did you notice that the Photographer isn't designated as a man or a woman? We usually assume a Photographer is a man and a Model a woman, but it would be really fascinating if the roles were reversed, wouldn't it? Man or woman, the Inner Voice would be you—the evil you, it appears.

So, what kind of a spot do you think this is—what's the concept, target market, tone, and manner, and what are you (both Photographer and Inner Voice, *and* the Model) doing in this commercial?

Well, this is certainly a Real-Life spot with a kinky bent to it, but it doesn't go to extremes other than to push the boundaries of human nature. We all listen to our inner voices, but, of course, we don't blindly turn into blithering idiots, either (unless we're in a TV spot).

Conceptually, this is about a person with a weakness for ice-cream novelties who's a slave to his or her inner voice. The Photographer has no resistance to inner *cravings*, which makes him or her, well, honest about what he or she wants. It's about giving in. This concept also creates an easy way to focus on the delicious, nearly sinful chunky fudge and crunchy peanuts that Dreamy Cream wants to feature. The story is linear.

The tone and manner are pretty "adult," wouldn't you say? Fashion shoots are typically sexy; we've got an Inner Voice with bad intentions, and a person yelling, "Give me nuts!" All of which points to our target market, which is: Adults who secretly love ice-cream novelties. And that's noteworthy because ice-cream advertising is usually directed towards kiddies. But Dreamy Cream felt that many adults secretly love those nut-covered ice-cream cones they ate when they were young.

Judging from what's emanating from the action, Dreamy Cream appears to have a brand personality that's delightfully out of control (which is an effect their products can have on people). Something about Dreamy Cream's personality says Jim Carrey or Robin Williams—do you agree?

It's pretty easy to see who's doing what in this ad. There's no smoke and mirrors here. The Inner Voice is setting off trip-mines in an attempt to play with the Photographer's head. The Photographer loves fudge and nuts to the extent of losing it in front of the Model. Together, they're selling the ice-cream cone. The Model needs to contribute to the authenticity of being a model in a room with a crazy person. The whole commercial is as nutty as the topping on the cone.

THE BUTTON

When you watch commercials you'll notice that many of them will end with a little scene that caps off the entire spot. Often the final shot of the product will appear, then this last scene. It's called the button. The Rita's ad has one and so does Dreamy Cream.

This is the button for this chapter.

Someday you'll be handed a script, and after looking at it for awhile, you'll be able to use it like a road map to get you to a place where you know how to fit into the commercial. The map will point out traps to avoid. You'll be able to make a bona fide choice about what you're going to do with your character. Eighty percent of the people in the waiting area with you won't know how to read the map.

Enjoy the trip.

⑧ Storyboards

If a script is a road map, then a storyboard will give you the topography.

A storyboard is like a comic book. It's an illustrated version of the script, highlighting key visual moments in the story—a graphic guide—that serves a couple of basic purposes. Just like a comic book, its main function is to tell the story in an exciting and provocative manner. It's also used to present the concept of the commercial in broad visual strokes to the client (because clients usually don't think in visual terms), and, in the process, explain the commercial, clarify details, and give the client an idea of how much it's going to cost to produce the spot. And, it's used to present the concept to production companies in a broad visual manner to see if the director is interested in directing the spot. If so, the production company will perform a cost estimate and send that bid to the agency for consideration. When available, boards are also sent to casting directors so they can understand the commercial a little better.

> **TIP:** *A storyboard is an illustrated version of the script.*

Unfortunately, they aren't created specifically for actors, and that's one reason why they don't show up at calls that often.

Storyboards can help clarify a concept, the execution, and other fine points, but beware that, by the time you see one, the commercial may have gone through some changes that *aren't reflected* in the board you're staring at. The board may still be an original, but budget restrictions, client meddling, and numerous other factors might alter scenes and camera shots, creating changes you may not be aware of. The simple reason for this is—you guessed it—money. Boards are divided into frames, and storyboard artists charge by the frame. Making changes costs money. Occasionally, ad agency art directors will draw boards to keep costs down, but the funny thing is, *most art directors aren't artists!* (That's why they're called art *directors.*) With some notable exceptions, most of them can't draw anything more than rudimentary stick figures. And therefore storyboard execution remains in the capable, expensive hands of real artists.

Soooo, when it comes to looking at storyboards, you must keep an open mind. That board may not be completely up to date.

If you're fortunate when you arrive at the casting facility, a black-and-white photocopy of the original board will be taped up on the wall near the sign-in area, or there may be a stack of them on the sign-in desk for you to snag. (If you don't see one, ask.) The board at the initial call will be the closest to the original action of the spot. The one at the callback will be the one more likely to have changed, and if you think something has changed that could affect your part, ask the casting director.

Bottom line: refer to the board, but stick to the script.

> **TIP:** *The storyboard you find at either call may not be up to date.*

STORYBOARD ELEMENTS

For the sake of brevity, cost, and covering all the bases, ad agencies pack every frame of a board with as much information as possible. Each frame is considered to be a shot, but in reality it might take a lot of shots to accomplish the action of one frame. Most boards average about eight to ten frames; some are longer (especially for vignette-style commercials), but many are shorter, resulting in what are called "key frames," in which the action is compacted down to its most important elements.

In order for the client to better comprehend the action, facial expressions and physical movement depicted by the characters are sometimes way over the top. Don't try to emulate them. You'll never be able to smile that wide, cry that hard, or jump that high.

> **TIP:** *Don't attempt to emulate big facial or physical expressions.*

Depending on whether the storyboard is laid out vertically or horizontally, you'll see that underneath or next to each image area is a window containing character dialogue, stage directions, and sometimes an important bit of information about the shot. Your character should correspond to the one in the script. If it doesn't, ask.

Don't worry if the character doesn't look like you.

> **TIP:** *Don't worry if the way the character is drawn doesn't look exactly like you.*

Arrows are often drawn on the image to indicate the direction of camera moves such as a pan, zoom, push, or dolly (details below). These arrows are there to remind the director that the agency wants to highlight a piece of action or glamorize the product. Directors take these arrows or notes under consideration and come up with better camera moves when they create their shooting board or when they get on the set.

Often a sentence or some kind of graphic will be superimposed over the action in the image area. These are the supers mentioned earlier and you see them on TV all the time. When it's a price point (Now Only $99!), or the name of the advertiser, or anything that's providing sales or other advertising information, most of the time you can ignore it. But if the super appears to be part of the concept of the spot, then check it out. For instance, HE'S SO SMART could be floating at the bottom of the scene you're in, but the character you're reading for is actually very stupid. Be careful and keep your eyes peeled for supers that say one thing, when the action says another.

> **TIP:** *Supers may say one thing, but the action may say another.*

Musical directions can get in the way unless you're dancing, singing, or moving to music. In "music-driven" commercials there will be a boom box in the audition studio blasting out the beat or providing cues.

And finally, as a general rule, the way shots are framed shouldn't concern you at an audition. But as you'll learn, there are certain instances when knowing your framing can be helpful.

EVERY PICTURE TELLS A STORY

The board should reinforce your understanding of the concept of the commercial that you've derived from the script.

Use the visual clues in the storyboard to *clarify* elements of the commercial, but unless there's no script—and that sometimes happens—don't use it as your absolute guide. If you get confused, put it aside and use the script or the directions you've received from the casting people.

> **TIP**: *The best use for a storyboard is to clarify elements of the commercial.*

Here are some things you might discover. First, you may be able to get a feel for the flow of the action and the pace of the commercial. Watch how the action flows from frame to frame, because, like so many spots you've studied on TV, the action may be nonlinear and disjointed, and that kind of jumping around can affect the transitions you'll make if your character appears throughout the story. The action can also influence your behavior if you only appear once. Or, you may identify shots that your character doesn't appear in which could agitate your character's behavior.

You can get a sense of the actual location. You'll know that you're in a castle courtyard, or in a restaurant, on a busy sidewalk, or in the tiny kitchen of a five story walk-up, and you'll be able to make a decision about how that environment is going to guide your behavior. The frames could also show that you're going to appear in different places, too. Shadows and lighting can indicate the time of day.

You'll find out where you are in space—in relationship to the other performers.

It's possible to glean some info about relating to the background atmosphere, too. (People in crowd scenes used to be called extras, now they're politely called background atmosphere. Many of these people make their living solely from this type of work. They deserve your respect.) For instance, your character is situated in a rowdy crowd at an arm-wrestling competition. So you ask yourself, "How do I behave in this crowd? Am I in the middle of the crowd or out in front of them? Are they reacting to me?"

> TIP: *A storyboard can open the door to a commercial and show you where you live.*

You'll take note that you have a dog, or you're holding a prop. You'll know if you're standing, sitting, walking, or whatever.

The board will always make the brand, the product, or the service the star of the show, and it's up to you to determine a natural relationship with the star.

If it's a non-dialogue spot with a VO carrying the ball, pay very close attention to what it's saying. The VO may say one thing, but your action could be ironically different.

SAMPLE FRAMES

The next few pages contain individual storyboard frames that represent some of the more common storytelling situations we've discussed above. There's no way this little sampler of frames will give you a master's in "frameology," but it should at least help you get familiar with some basic information individual frames can impart. Since the same storyboard artist drew all these, his style may make it appear that they're from the same commercial, but they're not. These frames are for stand-alone demonstration only. We'll get to a couple of full-blown storyboards shortly.

If you'd like to look at a lot of naked frames (sans scripts) go to *www.famousframes.com* or *www.frameworks-la.com*. Click on the various artists and you'll get an eyeful of styles and techniques, plus reference on some of the topics below.

Ready? Let's roll a few frames.

Just like our first frame (figure 1), a good opening frame can help you with a *sense of place*. An illustration like this can illuminate a video instruction in the script and give your imagination a jolt. For instance, the video instruction for this shot merely says: OPEN ON MEDIEVAL-CASTLE COURTYARD. If your only point of reference was a script, you could

Figure 1

probably dream up an interesting location. But this frame is jumping with activity, not to mention the size of the place. How you'd act in a big, bustling, robust arena like this would certainly be different than the puny image you may have invented from the script.

In addition to providing a sense of place, one of the cool things about a storyboard is that it only takes one frame to colorfully establish a *mood*. Take a look at figure 2. The script notation for this shot says: HE ENTERS A SEEDY HOTEL ROOM. But, wow, the way that shot looks could give you much, much more to feed off of.

Figure 2

Figure 3

As this frame above (figure 3) illustrates, you can discover *who's in the scene with you*, and not only that, but how their demeanor, action, reaction, and approximation could affect you. For some reason, there's also a dog in this shot. You'd want to know why.

You'll often see frames where *character action* is strongly emphasized, like in the next two frames (figure 4 and figure 5). Big gestures like Granny thrusting her cookies at the camera, and the guy furtively looking around are indicated mainly to stress an important physical

Figure 4

Figure 5

action or to highlight a turning point in the commercial. Shots are commonly rendered like this because the agency doesn't want anyone to miss that moment.

Another way to indicate character action or movement is with arrows, like you see in these frames (figure 6 and figure 7). These arrows aren't subtle, and that's so nobody misses the point that the guy is *moving* in a certain direction to catch the vase, or that a woman storms past the desks and out of the office.

Figure 6

Figure 7

Don't confuse the arrows in figure 8, figure 9, and figure 10 with the previous arrows shown that indicate character movement or action. These demonstrate *camera moves* and *camera direction*. For instance, that arrow wrapping around the character in the first frame calls for a pan across her face. Those arrows in the companion frame demonstrate a "push in" to the subject from a wide shot to a medium close-up. The two guys are running as the camera dollies along with them. In an audition,

Figure 8

Figure 9

it's a safe bet to ignore the camera move arrows because the camera rarely moves in the studio. It is better to concentrate on your performance.

TIP: *Most camera moves indicated by arrows won't actually happen at an audition.*

Here are two examples of something emphasized earlier. Figure 11 and figure 12 are examples of *over-the-top emotion*. Remember that quite

Figure 10

Figure 11

often characters are depicted like this *for clients* so they have no doubt about what the character is doing. This doesn't mean that you should duplicate the cartoon person in the frame. First do it your way, and then allow the director to craft your performance.

A *tight close-up* (figure 13) is usually a good indication that something important is happening to your character at that moment. If you see a series of tight close-ups on the board, that means they intend to

Figure 12

Figure 13

shoot in a very intimate style. In that case, you'll need to harness your ability to speak volumes with small expressions.

This next frame (figure 14) is an example of a *key moment*. Obviously something important is going on at this moment in the spot. This type of frame is closely related to what are called "key frames." Sometimes a board will boil the whole show down to its primary concern with just one or two key frames.

Figure 15 is an example of a *tight close-up on a piece of business*, which is much different than a close-up of your face. When small events like flipping a light switch, buttering a scone, or picking out red

Figure 14

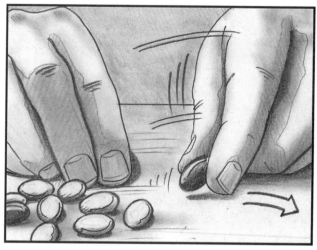

Figure 15

jujubes are highlighted with their own frames, it means they're important. Often, a hand model will be hired to perform specialized tasks because hand models are really good at intricate, umm, handiwork. But even if a hand model does the close-up work, *those are still your hands*, so pay attention to the shot. (More on this in chapter 11.)

These last two frames are no-brainers. Figure 16 is of a person holding or using a product with a super in the frame. A super is treated as an element in a shot just the same as any product, person, or scenic detail. On

Figure 16

Figure 17

the set, when the director of photography composes a shot that contains a super, he or she will consider its position in the frame, which could cause you to sit, stand, or move in a way to create room for the super to be placed in postproduction. But at the audition, all you should be concerned with is holding the product within the boundaries of the shot they've framed up with the video camera. Don't get hung up on the super.

> **TIP:** *Don't concern yourself with supers that deal with boiler-plate information like product names or prices.*

Finally, figure 17 is a medium close-up of someone taking a large bite into a sandwich or burger. You might get some idea of the degree of pleasure associated with eating a product from a frame, but once again, beware of an overblown reaction. Just pretend to eat naturally when they roll the tape. If they want it big, they'll tell you.

REVIEW BOARD

Before we break down a couple of storyboards it's good to remember that any one spot could be drawn many different ways. (Check out those Web sites.) As in comic books, attitude can influence the style of the drawings on the page.

And one more thing. It would be great to cover every nuance of every kind of board you'll ever encounter, but obviously that can't be achieved here. These exist simply so that those of you who aren't familiar with storyboards can get a taste of what one or two actually look like and how they operate. Maybe some of you more experienced actors might discover something to add to your audition arsenal as well.

First up is a board that's going to make you think a little bit, but hopefully not tax your powers of perception. Other than the always-important VO, there ain't no dialogue in this spot, therefore, no script. Just an eight-frame board.

BODACIOUS BURGERS

The advertiser is Bodacious Burgers, a chain famous for their "Big Ol' Burger." The main character is the Referee, so concentrate on him. (Apologies—ladies, the Referee could just as easily be a woman.) We'll pretend that you've been told that the part is a straight-looking guy in his mid-twenties and he's the referee of an arm-wrestling match in a bar, but that's about it. You're going to have to get most of your information from the board and the VO. (In chapter 9, you'll get some awesome tips about gathering more background information on commercials, such as directors' styles of shooting, but we're only going to discuss the bones of boards here.)

Have fun.

INT. HONKY TONK.
TWO BURLY GUYS ARE ARM WRESTLING,
SWEATING AND GRUNTING, NEITHER ONE
GAINING LEVERAGE.

THE CROWD IS HOOTIN' AND HOLLERIN'.

Storyboard illustrated by Marcus Endean.

REFEREE APPEARS IN FRONT OF CROWD
HOLDING A BODACIOUS BURGERS BAG AND
TAKES OUT A "BIG 'OL BURGER."

BEGIN MUSIC

REFEREE HOLDS THE BURGER OVER TO ONE
SIDE OF THE WRESTLERS AND THEIR ARMS
MAGNETICALLY MOVE AS ONE TO THAT SIDE.
CROWD LEANS IN UNISON.

CROWD: OOOH.

PLAYFULLY, HE SWINGS THE BURGER OVER TO THE OTHER SIDE. HELPLESSLY, THEIR ARMS MOVE TO THAT SIDE. CROWD LEANS WITH THEM.

CROWD: OOOH.

CUT TO PRODUCT SHOT OF BURGER

VO: It's the big temptation. The new Big 'Ol Burger from Bodacious Burgers. A third pound beef patty, crisp bacon, onion rings and our own Bodacious BBQ sauce.

REFEREE STANDS ABOVE HOLDING BURGER.
WRESTLER'S ARMS STRETCH UPWARD
TOGETHER TOWARD IT.

CROWD: AHHH.

CUT TO PRODUCT SHOT OF BURGER
SUPER: $1.99
MUSIC: BODACIOUS THEME
VO: Irresistible taste. Irresistible price.

REFEREE MOVES BURGER FROM SIDE TO SIDE AT AN UNATURALLY HIGH SPEED. WRESTLERS' ARMS WHIP BACK AND FORTH IN A BLUR.

VO: Bo DAY Shusss!

Dang! You shouldn't have had any trouble figuring out the action, style, and concept of this commercial. A Real-Life spot, to be sure, but pumped up to comic proportions. The concept? Easy. The Big 'Ol Burger is so tempting, it acts like a people magnet. (Heck, the Voice-Over even calls it "the big temptation.") The story? The Referee playfully tortures the powerless arm wrestlers with a burger, and the crowd loves it.

This board yields many informational diamonds as well. First off, you must've noticed that the bar where this arm-wrestling match is taking place seems like one of those barn-like joints that have a separate room just for the mechanical bull. Therefore, you wouldn't be working in a small space. You can also tell that these aren't two gentlemen arm wrestling over a beer or something. This looks like a big deal. And even though they go under the spell of the burger, somehow they comically stay locked together in combat throughout the whole spot. And look at the crowd. They're rowdy honky-tonk people—and they're close to you. There's a lot of energy indicated and a lot of good stuff to play off of.

See? Just by looking at the frames, you can get an idea of the place, the people in the spot with you, how you relate to them (the other cast members *and* the background atmosphere), and the story line. Most of this has been framed up as wide shots to accommodate action and movement. The lack of close-ups indicates that this isn't what you'd call a quiet commercial.

There's more.

Judging from the setting, the characters, and the action, you could surmise that the Bodacious-brand personality is down-home country. (Jeff Foxworthy would be great as the Referee.) At any rate, this spot doesn't connote "opera-going Mercedes owners." Although their main target market is obviously fast-food burger lovers, the board is giving off something that says that the real core market is more likely the NASCAR Nation. That's who they're talking to, and if you were the right type, that's why you'd be there. Obviously the bar, a rowdy crowd, a devilish referee (who doesn't do any refereeing at all!), and stupid arm wrestlers who elicit a feeling of, "Don't they get it!?" sum up the Bodacious tone and manner, which seem to be, "We're just funnin' with y'all." (You'd expect Bill Engvall to walk in and say, "Here's your sign.") The VO even provides a clue. The copywriter was kind enough to spell out the client's name with some phonetic swagger: *Bo Day Shusss.*

All of this should make you ask yourself how your character would behave in that environment. Oddly, the Referee is drawn with a sort of confident sereneness, and I think that's a clue to his comic counterpoint to all the craziness he creates, but how you'd behave would be up to you.

What are you doing in this spot? You've got the power of the burger. Everybody else (in their own way) feels the power of the burger. No hidden agenda here and nobody's getting used for any purpose other than supporting the message that this is one dee-licious, tempting burger.

And that's just from looking at the visuals. But what if you had a little more to go on?

AND NOW, A WORD FROM OUR SPONSOR

Let's take a quick break from our commercials to talk about the people responsible for them. Rita's Fajitas, AllerGood, and the rest are fictitious advertisers, but real or not, their scripts and boards have yielded a lot of good stuff to use based mostly on observation. But say for a moment that these were real brick-and-mortar companies. If they really existed, you might be familiar with their advertising from what you've seen on TV or heard on the radio. However, it's quite likely you wouldn't. For instance, you might live in Los Angeles and be totally in the dark about a southeastern burger chain called Bodacious. Or you may have a passing awareness of Dreamy Cream, but not much more than a hazy image of the brand. So, if you wanted to dig up some more useful factoids, what would you do?

Come on, you already know this. What's the quickest way to find out about a company? Go to their Web site! Yes! A quick trip to their site can give you all kinds of info you can use.

> **TIP**: *Advertisers' Web sites are treasure troves of inside info.*

Check out the way the site looks. Is it really cool? Really cold and corporate? Really video-game radical? Really boring? Maybe the language they use is colorful and the graphics are avant-garde. Maybe the language they use is dreary and the site has all the quality of one of those mini-mall bargain stores. Whatever, the ingenuity and creativity of the site—and the way it makes you feel—could be an indication of the company's brand personality. That's worth knowing. And there's other valuable info to dig up. Say the company is using their TV spot to introduce a new product or service to the world. Often companies will break the news on their Web site before they go on the air, and if you can get some inside dope on their new line of panty hose, or their new class of service, you're ahead.

But best of all, many large corporations will archive their TV spots, giving you a free history lesson on their brand.

If you're lucky, you can download a few ads and watch them one after another. Notice how the advertisements play as a campaign. Look for any theme or concept that runs through the campaign, and test for DNA. When a company has a tag line, see if the ads pay it off, or live up to its promise. Observe how the people behave. If there's anything else that jumps out at you, write it down. Then get a good night's sleep.

We now return to our regularly scheduled commercial.

MEGAPHONE

Ladies and gentlemen, it's the moment you've been waiting for! Yes, it's the MegaPhone commercial! Complete with script *and* storyboard. You didn't think we'd go to all this trouble discussing the creation of a MegaPhone ad without actually seeing it in the flesh, did you? No way.

The purpose of putting the MegaPhone script together with its companion storyboard is, first, to create an opportunity to see how a board can clarify and illuminate sketchy action and directions written in a script. And, second, to tie together all we've learned up to this point.

With a nod toward the next chapter, you'd have been informed that you'd be reading for the Businesswoman, described as "a young career woman, smart, athletic, and fearless." (Pay attention to the other two supporting parts as well. They have a lot to do with the concept.)

Now, read the script and try to visualize the action from scene to scene. See if you can understand what's going on. Then compare your perceptions with the storyboard. Afterwards, we'll go through the script and board scene by scene, and then finally talk about how the mechanics of the spot can work for you.

Just to remind you, all scripts aren't properly laid out like this one, with the Video instructions in ALL CAPS directly opposite the Audio instructions. (You should be so lucky.) When a script is set up like this, with paragraphs or sentences directly across from each other, each group constitutes a scene. Each of these scenes should correspond to a frame on the storyboard.

Okay, first give the script a shot. The storyboard follows right after it.

 Jenkins & Associates

MegaPhone :30 sec "Helicopter" 4/8/03
Rev# 3   Job # TM903   ISCI:
Prod: "Summer sign up"

VIDEO	AUDIO
OPEN ON: UPSIDE-DOWN CITY SKY-LINE MOVING BY FROM THE AIR.	SFX: WIND BUSINESSWOMAN OC: Wow! What a view!
BUSINESSWOMAN DANGLES UPSIDE DOWN BELOW HELICOP-TER FROM SEATBELT WRAPPED AROUND HER ANKLE. SHE'S HOLDS A CELLPHONE.	SFX: NOW WE HEAR CHOPPER MUSIC BUSINESSWOMAN: Wheeeee!
BUSINESSMAN IN HELICOPTER DOORWAY FROM HER POV.	BUSINESSMAN: Are you okay?
LOOKING UP TO BUSINESSMAN	BUSINESSWOMAN: I'm fine! I've got free roaming!
MEDIUM SHOT OF HER DIALING THE PHONE. SUPER: Free Roaming	VO: With MegaPhone, you always get free roaming -- wherever you are.
SHE SPEAKS INTO PHONE. THEN HOLDS IT OUT TOWARDS SKYLINE. SUPER: Free Video Messaging	BUSINESSWOMAN: Honey, loook! VO: And free video messaging.
CLOSEUP OF HER HUSBAND HOLD-ING PHONE WITH UPSIDE-DOWN SKYLINE IN VIDEO WINDOW. CUT TO: HUSBAND FAINTS. SUPER: No Sign-up Fee	VO: And if you get MegaPhone's unlimited minutes package before June thirtieth, there's no sign-up fee.
BUSINESSMAN AND WOMAN RE-UNITED ON TARMAC. HELICOPTER IDLES IN BG.	BUSINESSMAN: I thought you were going to lose it. BUSINESSWOMAN: Naw, I always have a good signal with MegaPhone. VO: There's that, too.
CUT TO: SEA OF HANDS HOLDING UP PHONES MEGAPHONE LOGO.	VO: Good call.

OPEN ON: UPSIDE-DOWN CITY SKYLINE MOVING
BY FROM THE AIR.
SFX: WIND
BUSINESSWOMAN OC: Wow! What a view!

BUSINESSWOMAN DANGLES UPSIDE DOWN
BELOW HELICOPTER FROM SEATBELT WRAPPED
AROUND HER ANKLE. SHE HOLDS A CELLPHONE.
SFX: NOW WE HEAR CHOPPER
MUSIC
BUSINESSWOMAN: Wheeeee!

Storyboard illustrated by Mardel Monet.

BUSINESSMAN IN HELICOPTER DOORWAY FROM HER POV.

BUSINESSMAN: Are you okay?

LOOKING UP TO BUSINESSMAN
BUSINESSWOMAN: I'm fine! I've got free roaming!

MEDIUM SHOT OF HER DIALING THE PHONE.
SUPER: Free Roaming

VO: With MegaPhone, you always get free roaming
-- wherever you are.

SHE SPEAKS INTO PHONE. THEN HOLDS IT OUT
TOWARDS SKYLINE.
SUPER: Free Video Messaging
BUSINESSWOMAN: Honey, loook!
VO: And free video messaging.

CLOSEUP OF HER HUSBAND HOLDING PHONE
WITH UPSIDE-DOWN SKYLINE IN VIDEO WINDOW.

VO: And if you get MegaPhone's unlimited minutes
package before June first, there's no sign-up fee.

CUT TO: HUSBAND FAINTS.
SUPER: No Sign-up Fee

BUSINESSMAN AND WOMAN REUNITED ON
TARMAC. HELICOPTER IDLES IN BG.
BUSINESSMAN: I thought you were going to lose it.
BUSINESSWOMAN: Naw, I always have a good signal
    with MegaPhone.
VO: There's that, too.

CUT TO: LOTS OF HANDS HOLDING UP PHONES.
MEGAPHONE LOGO

VO: Good call.

Whew. This is a big-budget commercial. The agency has somehow managed to sell the client a small movie featuring a helicopter, aerial photography, a stuntperson, computer-assisted effects, two locations (not including the sky), and three talents. Cool.

Now let's see what's going on.

The Video instruction in the first scene of the script says OPEN ON: UPSIDE-DOWN CITY SKYLINE MOVING BY FROM THE AIR. This description of the establishing shot might be hard to comprehend as written because we're not used to seeing upside-down cities flying by, but the first frame of the storyboard shows us all we need to know. The SFX tells us that we don't hear the helicopter yet, only the wind rushing by. The Businesswoman speaks Off Camera (OC) before we see her.

Even if you didn't have a board, the second scene of the script should clarify the situation: Somehow this woman has fallen out of a helicopter, dangling from her seatbelt. But look how frame two of the board really punches up the drama of our lady's predicament. She's *way* up there, zooming past tall buildings. Neither the script nor the board tells us how she fell out of the helicopter. Why? Because it's not important to the commercial. In fact, it would get in the way. She's just there.

Visually there's nothing shown providing any detail about the seatbelt. They would film a cutaway to a Close-Up of the buckle wrapped around her ankle, but that's not indicated here.

Next, both script and board establish her distressed colleague in the doorway of the helicopter, but once again, the frame helps to dramatize the seriousness of the situation, plus give us a radical shot from the Businesswoman's Point of View (POV).

Frame four is a very telling shot for you. Here she is, upside down, smiling and giving a thumbs-up while answering her colleague's question. The script tersely says, "LOOKING UP TO BUSINESSMAN." This frame says a whole lot more.

In scenes five and six, she calls her husband and uses the video feature of the phone. That action tracks nicely, but then scene seven suddenly cuts away to her husband in a different location. The script doesn't say where, but the board shows us (and the guy who'd come in to audition for the Husband) that this action takes place in an office. This cutaway to the office is important because, even though they're never seen (or don't audition) together, the Husband has to have a relationship with his Businesswoman wife. The little arrow is a camera move to indicate a quick jump from a Close-Up of his wife in the phone to him passed out on the floor. If you were the actor auditioning for the Husband, you could ignore this arrow.

Finally, in frame nine, everyone is back safely on the ground and the Businesswoman and her coworker trade dialogue. Judging from the frame, the tarmac could be anywhere a helicopter would land. Anyway, you'd be outdoors.

The last frame is the MegaPhone logo above a sea of hands holding phones. There's nothing in this shot that relates back to the concept, so you wouldn't bother with it.

One interesting aspect of this spot is the way the dialogue is used to talk about the product features like free roaming. Even though they'd be shouting to be heard (you realized that, didn't you?), their exchange comes off as a conversation. He yells, "Are you okay?" She responds with, "I'm fine! I've got free roaming." That's very crafty—and a staple of commercials—but just to make sure we don't miss these product features, supers highlighting them appear throughout. In this spot, none of the supers are ironic or facetious, just straightforward info.

So now we have a pretty good idea about what's going on from scene to scene in this commercial. We can see how the spot flows, its drama, its camera moves, etc. Most important, you have a more coherent picture of what you're actually *doing*.

Now let's tie this all together. But to do so, we'll have to utilize a familiar filmmaking technique called a flashback.

If you had the luxury of going to Megaphone's Web site before the audition, you could also see some of the throughput of their brand in this ad. You might have been able to pick up on a couple of things that would give you some hints about the personality of this spot, and maybe your personality in it as well. So, just for a moment let's time travel back to the day before your audition and visit MegaPhone's site.

As a "Monday morning quarterback," you'll realize that what you'd discover there contains elements found in the helicopter commercial—elements that are the offspring of the basic tenets set down in the ad agency's creative brief back in chapter 4.

RIPPLE DISSOLVE TO: The day before your audition.

Because their site doesn't actually exist, allow me to point out the sights.

Their site has a modern, cutting-edge look and feel about it, but it doesn't smell like a giant corporation is behind it. Maybe that has something to do with the way it's designed and the easygoing, conversational style of expressing information that gives you the *impression* that this is a friendly company. There's a navigation button labeled "MegaTales," and a click takes you to a page filled with true stories about users getting out of jams with MegaPhone wireless features.

On their home page, there's a picture of a bunch of young businessmen and women who look like they're having a good time. Next to the picture is a big blurb announcing, "No sign-up fee if you contract for our unlimited minutes package." This may or may not be the product they're going to feature in the TV commercial, but the people in the picture sure look like they could be your contemporaries.

Lucky you—MegaPhone has a library of their commercials. You remember some of them, and as you roll through each one, you notice that they advertise to a number of target markets—teen cell phone-aholics, families, young businesspeople on the go—and although each spot has a different tone and manner to cater to these groups, a theme runs through the entire campaign. It seems that people who use MegaPhone are plucky in the face of wild or adverse situations. (In one spot a teen downloads music to her phone that she plays back to calm down a deranged ape.) You also notice that the spots are very movie-like. In other words they use action to tell the story, the dialogue is minimal but clever, and there aren't any monologues. The music is quirky and fresh and in some cases runs counterpoint to the action.

You've figured this out, haven't you?

The site and the ads all live and breathe the *spunky* brand personality of "a very personable company with a 'do anything to help you' spirit" spelled out in the creative brief in chapter 4. The wild and adverse situations are molded after their trademark "performing with a sense of humor under any circumstances" concept that appears in each of their commercials. That's the reason for the site's MegaTales, and it's the concept of this commercial as well: A woman is dangling from a flying helicopter. She uses the opportunity to cheerfully call her husband and give him an incredible sightseeing tour. In the process, she's actually giving a Product Demo of MegaPhone calling features. (The VO provides the hook for the deal.) She could be sitting in an outdoor cafe and say basically the same things, but that wouldn't be very fun or engaging, would it? She wouldn't be very *plucky* talking to us over a cappuccino—especially to a target market of on-the-go, young businesspeople. By putting her in a whacked-out predicament, the agency not only continues to stress MegaPhone's brand personality, but retains the tone and manner for all of their advertising, too.

You see how all this fits together. And it all relates to your performance, too.

For instance, from what you know now, do you think you'd play the businesswoman as being terrified? No. If she was wet-your-panties afraid, it would go against everything the MegaPhone brand stands for. Wrong choice.

Which leads me to this thought: Even if you have a strong notion of how you'd play her, there's one mistake you'd want to avoid in the audition studio, and that'd be physically trying to perform upside down. Honest to goodness, if this was a real spot, I bet we'd see actors come in and try reading this while standing on their heads or draped backwards over a chair. If you booked the spot, you'd be hanging upside down in front of a blue screen matte until your face turned red. But you definitely wouldn't want to duplicate the action at the audition because, number one, it will distract you from performing, and two, the director will think you're a buffoon. (Much more on this later.)

Well, as the director says when a film or commercial is finished shooting, "That's a wrap." And that wraps up this section on scripts and boards. Next, your total immersion into the real world of booking a job.

9 Good Things to Know before You Audition

Your audition begins long before you ever set foot in a studio. Here's a primer on getting the right information, what to wear, what not to wear, how to prepare, and, above all, how to make yourself comfortable for those all-so-crucial three minutes we've set aside just for you.

YOU'LL RARELY SEE A SCRIPT IN ADVANCE

You may be familiar with the practice of actors getting to see the "sides" a day or so before a film, sitcom, or episodic TV audition so they can rehearse on their own, but don't expect this treatment in the commercial business. Sometimes, if a script is a laundry list of product attributes or contains complex terminology, then your representative may have one available to fax to you, but that's rare. So, bank it that most of the time *you'll never see a commercial script until you arrive at a casting call.* That's why it's very important to know how to interpret scripts and storyboards and be able to apply your knowledge in that crucial half hour before you go in and read.

> **TIP:** *You'll never see a commercial script in advance.*

IT'S YOUR CALL

Good news. The phone rings. You pick it up. Well, whaddya know, you're being called to audition for a TV commercial.

So now what do you do?

Pay close attention to the voice on the line, because in addition to learning the time and place of the audition and the name of the casting director, this is also your opportunity to get the lowdown on a couple of aspects of the commercial that can affect your performance.

Generally, an agent, or whomever it is with the power to get you into an audition, will say something like, "Can you be at Chelsea Studios tomorrow at 1:45 for a Budweiser commercial?" Or, "I've got a MegaPhone spot reading on Wednesday; are you available?" Most of the time, they'll phrase the information in that fashion. But if they don't include the name of the advertiser, ask who it is. If they don't tell you *what's* being advertised—a product or a service—find that out, too. This is imperative because now, for one, by studying commercials and keeping up on what's on the air these days, you've gained knowledge that may give you a slight indication of the type of spot you'll be reading for. By merely watching TV, you could surmise: Budweiser = beer = something funny like their current campaign. Okay, cool—that's almost a no-brainer. But even if you know a few tidbits about the advertiser, as you now so cleverly do, that alone isn't enough information to be useful. That means a trip on the Internet, and, as was the a case for our previous discussion, a look-see at MegaPhone's Web site. There's always a chance to extract some goodies about a product and download a couple of commercials.

All right, to continue with your phone call, you'll absolutely need to know the part you're reading for. The person on the line will probably volunteer what it is. If this were the MegaPhone ad the information you'd hear would go something like, "a young businesswoman, smart, athletic, and fearless." Good enough? Maybe.

Troy Evans says you should take it a step further. "You really need to know as much about the commercial as possible. What's the character? What's the ad campaign going to be like? If they're looking for a short-order cook, is it a dead-serious short-order cook, a Three Stooges short-order cook, or a Marlon Brando cook? You try to get that kind of information so you know how to prepare."

> **TIP:** *Get as much information about the part as you can.*

So now you've learned the advertiser (MegaPhone), the product (in this case, wireless service), the type of person they're looking for (a businesswoman type), and a hint of personality (smart, athletic, and fearless). Even though it's pretty easy to deduce that you'd wear a suit or business clothes to this audition, please make sure you're *clear* about their instructions. Say you're a guy and the caller simply says something colorful like, "You're a pirate." Suddenly your head is going, "Arrrgh, I know what a pirate is, matey!" and you'd have a vision of a swash-buckling cutthroat. But if that's *all* they say—just "a pirate"—then you'd better get more details. You'd hate to show up and find out they were casting for the *Pittsburgh* Pirates. Arrrgh, ya damn fool!

If the caller forgets or doesn't mention anything at all about the role, *ask about it!*

> **TIP:** *Don't be afraid to ask questions about the role. Better to be embarrassed now than later in front of a casting director.*

This is also an opportunity to find out if this is a part you can *actually play*. Nine times out of ten you're being called because of your look or a known ability. But if the part requires some special skill or ability, your agent or whoever's on the phone should let you know about it. He'll prob-ably ask, "Can you tap-dance? Juggle? Surf? Chug a twenty-four-ounce cola?" just to make sure. But if for any reason there's some requirement or aspect of the part that bugs you, get the details.

There is one more thing you should find out about the commercial, and this is crucial:

Who's the director?

For sure. It will be infinitely more helpful if you know something about the director's style and the kind of spots he directs before you go to the initial call. It will be especially helpful if you have some background when the time comes to face him or her at a callback, not to mention the shoot.

> **TIP:** *Do your best to find out who's directing the commercial, then use the Internet to find examples of his or her work.*

How important is this? Well, even directors want you to find out who's directing. Here are two of their opinions:

"It's really worth checking out what the director does. It's very easy to ask your agent for the name of the director and the company that he works for. In a matter of minutes you can go to this company's Web site and you can see the director's work. By the time you've entered the casting studio you know the sensibility of that director, you know his tastes, you know what amuses him. Every respectable production company has a site where a director's work can be seen. Now, it doesn't matter how carefully you plan to outwit or outsmart the director, because ultimately the director is looking for a face, a character that fits the script he's trying to direct. And even if the talent meet those criteria it can always be that the director will be overruled by the agency."

Now that's an interesting piece of advice from a very experienced director. He wants actors to be familiar with his work, but remain open to the possibility that anything can happen. And, as you'll see from the comments of this next director, a little bit of knowledge can not only give you clues about the spot you're going to read for, but also go a long way towards creating a better relationship with a director.

"Most people know nothing [about directors]. I'll be with actors who've been on a set with a director and they won't even remember his name.

"It's not a bad idea to speak to the casting director or have your agent speak to the casting director and ask, 'What *types* of spots does this guy do? Is he a comedy director? Is he a drama director? Is he a people director?' You're not questioning, 'is this [spot] supposed to be funny or no't,—*it's just so that you have an idea*. So, if you go in with a director who's known for comedy spots, *the chances are, it's going to be a comedy spot!* Which'll just give you more confidence. You don't have to do a lot of research. Get your agent to do a little work for you. Get him to get you information. Just so you have a little bit of knowledge. So, if a guy's a kid's director and he goes in and he's talking to you like a child and you're saying to yourself, 'Why's he talkin' to me like a child!?' Well, the guy *normally directs kids,* so at least you'd get it! It's not because he thinks you're immature or childlike."

TIP : *With a little research, you could enter the casting studio knowing the director's sensibility, his tastes, and what amuses him.*

If your agent doesn't know who's directing, he or she may know who the production company is, and that's just as valuable. You can track down production companies on the Web by going to one of the *411 Directories* that cater to the industry. Go to either *www.la411.com* or *www.newyork411.com* and click on "Production Companies and Ad Agencies." Unfortunately you'll have to scroll from one company to the next to see each one's list of directors, but when you find who you're looking for, click on the company link. When you get to the production company's site, you'll usually be able to view some of your director's spots and may even get a blurb about him or her. Be aware that the *411* sites aren't that up to date.

The best place to find out about directors, view their reels, and stay on top of current commercials is at *CreativeChannel* (*www.fastchannel.com/creativechannel*), which is part of the *FastChannel* network. This site is a major industry resource. They have over 45,000 TV commercials and videos available to view, along with a who's who of credits. Although this is a rather pricey subscription site, it is money well spent.

Many directors have their own sites, and it's pretty easy to type in their name in the browser and start searching. Short of that, here are some other sources:

You can search the database of the Directors Guild of America for free. It is at *www.dga.org*.

AdCritic (*www.adcritic.com*) is also a subscription site, but really worth it. It is all about current TV commercials, directors, and production companies. Subscribe to it and you also get a monthly copy of *Creativity* magazine mailed to you.

The *Source Maythenyi* (*sourcetv.com*) is also a top-notch site for directors and commercials. It's fee based.

Okay, let's continue. You jot down the info and hang up the phone. Fire up your computer, visit the MegaPhone Web site to get some background on the company, and then surf over to the Humungo Pictures site to bone up on Steam, the guy who's going to direct the spot. (Lately, a lot of directors have adopted the use of one name, like fashion models. Go figure.)

Get it, got it, good. The game is on. But if you think you're ready to play, there's another important decision to make before you go to the call.

YOUR UNIFORMS

You're a woman in your thirties, athletic, and attractive. You've been called to audition for a corporate-finance officer. What do you wear? You open your closet to a special rack of clothes, flick across the hangers, and your hand stops at a tailored suit. "I've got just the thing," you think confidently.

Or you've been called for a part that requires you to be out playing golf with your regular foursome.

"I've got it."

Or a part described as a frazzled after-school Mom.

"I've got it."

You're a guy in your early fifties, thick hair turning silver, stocky, with smiling eyes. You get a call for the part of a bank officer. What do you wear? You open your closet to a special rack of clothes and pull the plastic bag off a dark-blue pinstripe suit. "I've got it," you think confidently.

Or you've been called to be a guy who takes his dog out to the park to meet his buddies on a cool fall morning.

"I've got it."

Or a peewee-league football coach.

"Got it."

TIP: *Have at hand a specialized set of wardrobe just for auditions.*

Bernard Hiller suggests that every commercial actor have three or four "uniforms" in the closet that would work for the types they usually go out for. These are special clothes that are only worn to auditions. That's right, only for auditions, and there are a couple of excellent reasons for this. Number one, these are clothes that you've specially selected for yourself because they're what the ad agency is looking for. You look right wearing these clothes. Take the tailored suit, for example. Our actor has chosen a suit that looks just like the kind of suit a corporate-finance officer (or an attorney, or any other professional) would wear. It's what the agency expects to see. If she'd decided to wear a suit that was more trendy or hip (because she thought she'd look cool or feel better in that suit), she'd show up looking like a hip corporate-finance officer. However slight, this would be a disconnect for the agency.

Secondly, having a set of uniforms is going to become part of your ritual of getting ready for your audition. You'll understand when we discuss your ritual in a short while.

And finally, when you have a rack of clothes that all say "this actor looks right for the part," you can eliminate the doubt that comes with not being sure that you're wearing the right thing. You're going to be more confident. As you're hearing over and over in this book, agencies and directors love confident people.

When you start to pull your collection of uniforms together, get opinions from people you trust—your acting teacher, people in your class—and ask, "is this me?" You must feel confident that these clothes express your USP. When you put on any one of these outfits, it should look like something you wear all the time.

> **TIP:** *Avoid jingly jewelry or anything that could be distracting.*

> **TIP:** *If you make it to the callback, wear the same clothes you wore to the audition. That little bit of recognition can go a long way.*

REMEMBER: WHAT YOU WEAR SHOULD SIMPLY *INDICATE* THE CHARACTER

Hang on now. Don't make yourself crazy by putting together an overly specific and extensive wardrobe. Most people in commercials are dressed pretty normal, so most of the time when you come in for a first call, you're probably going to wear street clothes.

But what about parts that could be considered more *characteristic*, like a chef or a bellhop or a surgeon? In cases like these the casting director should provide a white chef's toque or a bellhop's jacket or a surgeon's blue smock. Hopefully you'll be told ahead of time that there will be something on hand for you to wear. But, to be on the safe side, have some clothes available that you can use to indicate these characters. For instance, a white jacket could indicate a doctor, a dentist, a lab technician, a chef, or even a waiter. It's all you need.

TIP: *Don't let your clothes do the acting for you.*

Please resist the temptation of letting your clothes do the acting for you.

For example, let's say the part calls for a cowboy. Obviously something about you connotes cowboy, so you don't need to push it. You own a western hat? Okay, bring it. No cowboy hat? Then just wear some jeans and a denim jacket or a T-shirt. But for cryin' out loud, podnah, don't come in wearing chaps and spurs swinging a lariat, with a plug of Red Man in your cheek. You're an actor who "acts" aren't you? So be you being a cowboy. Remember, we want to see *you*. In the end, it's your personality that's going to get you noticed.

Here's a true story.

We were casting for someone to play an old-time railroad worker. You know, the guy who sits back there in the caboose and does whatever those guys who sit back in the caboose do. In this case he was supposed to drink coffee. Anyway, we chose a number of rugged-looking guys from the casting tape and called them in. A few had somehow found real denim railroad caps to wear or red kerchiefs, and that was fine. But then, halfway through the session, in shuffles this, well, apparition. This guy was dressed in overalls, face all covered with soot and dirt, and he had some kind of rope hanging around his neck. He was carrying a big (and he said authentic) railroad spike-drivin' hammer. He even had one of those red signal lamps with him and it was *lit*! Here was a character we originally liked on tape and the poor guy just made one of the biggest mistakes any actor can ever make at a commercial audition: He'd gone way over the top with his props and ridiculous getup. We could barely suppress our laughter. The director could barely suppress his exasperation, and if there was an actor buried somewhere under all that baggage, he didn't want to waste time finding him. Sure, the actor got to read. And then he died the silent, untold death of not getting the part.

> **TIP:** *When in doubt, just use your head and keep it simple. Let your clothes give us the idea that you can be this person we're looking for. Just* indicate *the character.*

Yes, there are extreme situations. Occasionally you'll see some really bizarro characters in commercials: Actors dressed up as dogs, or big pieces of fruit, or monsters. The best thing you can do when you get called for something like that is to come in wearing clothes allowing you to move freely and comfortably. Nine times out of ten, a dog costume head or something representational will be available at the session for you to put on.

A WORD ABOUT HATS AND COLORS

Don't forget that audition rooms are usually lit from above like a night game at Wrigley Field. If you wear a big hat (like a western hat) during the audition, it'll shadow your whole face and hide your eyes, and that's not a good thing for people who make their living with their faces. That goes for hats in general. Sometimes you're better off just holding it or setting it down. If you think it's necessary to wear one, here's a tip: keep it on for the start of your slate,* then take it off when you say your name. That way, we'll see what you look like with your hat off. Then push it back on your head so the bill doesn't cast too much of a shadow.

Never attend a casting session wearing red or black. If you're a woman, don't think wearing black is going to make you look slimmer,

---

*A slate is a brief videotaping of you saying your name before your audition is actually recorded. We'll focus on slating in chapter 11.

because the director is going to think, "She's wearing black because she's probably fatter than she appears." On video, black obliterates shape and texture, and you just come out as this black form that's difficult to see.

Never, *never* wear red; red bleeds on videotape.

Never wear revealing clothing unless the part demands it. It makes you look like you're trying too hard. I've had a couple of occasions where women came in wearing, well, let's call it "peek-a-boo" clothing. We didn't cast them.

YOUR RITUAL

No professional boxer steps into the ring without getting himself up for the fight. Win or lose, he'll get himself mentally focused by using techniques like visualization and positive self-imagery. He'll listen to music that puts him in fighting mode, and get physically prepared by shadowboxing to stay loose and break a sweat. It's all part of a step-by-step regimen he's designed to carry him beyond the moment when the first bell rings.

Watch professional golf on TV sometime and you'll notice the men and women players have pre-shot routines they employ before they hit the ball. Golfers have something to deal with on every shot: the gallery, thoughts about a last bad shot, sweat trickling down their groin, swing mechanics, or TV cameras. Routines help them to block out that stuff so they can just concentrate on swinging the club and hitting better shots

Do you do anything to get yourself mentally ready for a call?

If you don't, you should consider putting some kind of ritual together. Whether it takes twenty minutes or two hours, a ritual or a set routine can really help you block out distractions and get your head into a positive space so that when you walk in and pick up that script, you're already focused.

I can't tell you exactly what your ritual should be, because everybody is different. But you should incorporate things from your everyday life that energize you and put you into a positive state of mind. What do you eat? Do you take a hot bath? Go to the gym? On the train or the subway on the way over, what music is playing through your headphones that really makes you feel incredible or motivated? Do you play positive-thinking tapes in the car during your drive to the session? Find out what works for you.

A commercial audition isn't anything like a prizefight, but isn't the prize worth giving yourself an edge?

> **TIP:** *Find a method you can use to get yourself relaxed and focused.*

⑩ In the Waiting Area

You've fought the fast-lane maniacs up the sunbaked 405 and finally, mercifully, found a half-shaded parking spot.

The exhaust mixes with the snow as the bus pulls away and you hike your shoulder bag up protectively as you look for the address.

Past two panhandlers and up the stoop is a steep narrow stairway that smells familiar, like a school lunchroom.

You trek across the searing parking lot.

The snow swirls around the numbers over the entrance.

You can hear your heart as you climb the green stairs.

You reach the door. You take a deep breath, and go in.

WHAT TO EXPECT

For those of you who've never been to a commercial call before, there's only one word that can describe what waits on the other side of that door: Bedlam.

Like any waiting area for an audition, it's filled with adrenaline and dreams. But this is different—it is not the hushed atmosphere that exists before you go in at South Coast Rep and Long Wharf or the Manhattan Theatre Club—but more like the waiting area for Southwest Airlines at Thanksgiving.

When you walk through the door, you're going to encounter a big waiting room filled with actors milling around, talking, murmuring, rehearsing, and schmoozing as they wait to be called into one of the smaller audition studios. There could be as many as ten casting sessions going on at once. They may be casting for little kids, and they're *really* noisy. You must find a way to relax yourself and concentrate. Maybe one good way to focus is to extend your ritual into this part of your experience.

THE DIFFERENCE BETWEEN THE INITIAL CALL AND A CALLBACK

The initial call (or first call) is one step up from a cattle call.

If you're a newbie or the casting director doesn't know you, and the part is a nonspeaking role, sometimes, your audition may be a taped interview with the casting director. Longtime Los Angeles casting director Susie Kittleson advises actors to beware of a "little chat" like this. This isn't a casual interview; it's actually an audition. While she's asking questions and getting to know you, she'll also be checking you out to see if you've got the right stuff. Just like at a job interview, you'll want to be relaxed and show that you have something valuable to bring to the job. If you've never gone through one of these mini auditions, you can anticipate the situation by holding mock interviews with a friend or your spouse. Allow them to ask very hard questions about your career and your abilities. Get yourself ready.

> **TIP:** *First-time interviews with casting directors are auditions, too.*

At the initial call, everybody's performance is videotaped back to back, wham-bam-thank-you-ma'am, by a casting assistant (rarely the casting director, unless it's your interview). It's a factory: You come in, they roll tape, you slate, read, and out you go. You'll pretty much get one shot at a read, maybe two, with minimal direction. You'll be pretty much on your own.

The callback, however, is an initial call on steroids.

The agency people and the director are all there in the room, up close and personal. You'll walk in, and . . . well, hang on, we'll get heavy into callbacks in chapter 13.

COMMON SENSE

Please arrive early enough to your call to allow yourself time to find out what studio you'll be in and to study the script and storyboard and get focused. 'Nuff said.

If you're running late or stuck in traffic, or you're just not going to make it, phone your agent or representative and have her call the casting facility for you. Never call the casting agent personally. You won't make friends that way.

Like I said, kids are often there to read for parts, too. They're there for a reason. But unless you've been called for a part that requires you to bring your child or baby with you, I highly recommend that you don't bring very young children to an audition. Cranky babies can be a major distraction. We've had moms bring kids inside the studio with them at the callback. Let me tell you, it's really hard for us to concentrate with a crying baby in the room. If you absolutely must bring your little one, see if you can arrange to have a friend come along to help babysit while you study your part and go in.

STANDARD PROCEDURE

When you show up for either an initial call or a callback, a couple of standard events take place. In the waiting area you'll sign in and then fill out a small form (the "size sheet") that asks you about your height, weight, sizes, and such. At some point they may take a Polaroid of you and attach it to the size sheet. When your name is called you'll take those inside, along with your headshot. (Keep extra headshots on hand just in case another casting director spots you in the lobby and says, "Do you have an extra headshot? I'm casting for something you'd be perfect for." P.S.: your picture should look like you.)

Then, pick up a script and look for your part. If you're lucky, a barely legible photocopy of the storyboard will be attached to the script or taped to the wall, or there may not be one. If you don't see one, ask the person in charge if any are available. As a matter of fact, this is a good time to ask questions.

QUESTIONS YOU CAN AND CAN'T ASK

Common sense says don't go overboard with questions. But many actors make the mistake of not asking *any* questions. They either don't know *what* to ask or they're afraid to ask because they don't want to appear foolish by asking the wrong questions. Either way, they're screwing themselves, because on the battlefield of an audition, the landscape is always changing. Actors who ask the right questions are going to put themselves in a better position to win.

Actors who know which questions to avoid don't get themselves in hot water, either. Let's start with the "Don't Asks," which can apply to the initial read and callbacks.

Don't Ask

Don't ask acting questions like, "What's my motivation?" and jazz like that. You're talking to a casting director, not Uta Hagen.

If you're lucky enough to have another call somewhere else and you're running late, and you start asking the casting director if you can be moved up, or you get all antsy and ask, "How long is this going to take?" or, "What's going *on* in there?!" you will not earn anything but grief.

It's a matter of respecting your fellow actors, too. If you're running late, call your agent and ask her to push back your next call. Or make it nice by asking an actor ahead of you if you can go in. After you've been in the audition pool for awhile, you'll most likely see the same people at calls, and you'll kind of know each other, so it should be okay to ask if you can go ahead. If that happens, tell the casting director about the change.

What to Ask at the Initial Call

I've mentioned that casting directors rarely attend first calls (unless they want to get to know you and tape your little "get-to-know-you" chat), and there's a good reason for this. They're either on the phone with ad agencies and talent agents, or they're running callback sessions that require their ultimate attention since the agency and director are in the house. They're often doing all these things at the same time, so they leave first calls to their assistants. There are usually two assistants: One outside in the lobby, wrangling the herd, and the video operator inside the studio.

The lobby assistant (or the casting director) should answer two very important questions for you:

One: Ask, "When is this shooting?" You've got to know if you'll be available on shoot day. If you have some sort of conflict with a possible shooting date, then it really doesn't make any sense to go in and read. There's nothing worse for an agency to go through the whole callback process and find out that a person we desire isn't available. That starts a domino effect: Now, out of fear, our back-up talent suddenly doesn't look as good as we originally thought, and we're confronted with the grim possibility of starting all over again. Grrr.

Two: Ask, "When are the callbacks being held?" If you're not going to be available for the callback, the casting director is going to wonder, "Why should we bother with auditioning you?" and you should politely excuse yourself. If you insist on auditioning, anyway, the casting director is going to feel you're wasting his or her time. You may also think it's a good idea not to mention your time conflict, and go ahead and read just for the experience. But if you get called back—knowing you can't make it—you'll only feel guilty.

> **TIP:** *Be sure to find out when the callback is being held and when the spot is shooting.*

If you have a question about the script, it's okay to ask one of the assistants basic questions. But know this: Casting assistants are often actors just like you. They aren't good sources of information because (a) their information is secondhand, and (b) they may sneak a chance to read for the same part, *so why should they tell you anything?*

Or, this from Troy Evans: "Personally, especially at the initial call, I try to avoid asking [them] questions because what you have is some unemployed actor who's being paid five dollars an hour to operate that camera, and I really don't want his point of view in my performance. Because, chances are, he doesn't know any more about that commercial than I do. And I've worried about that: you go in and do what may or may not get the job, but [what] you think is a respectable presentation of what you have in your mind, which is all an actor can do. But then you go in—and this happens a lot—and this guy says, 'No, no. Do it like you have an uncle in Poughkeepsie who drinks.' They give you all this bizarre direction that comes out of *their* particular world and whatever acting class *they're* taking at the time. And they may very well be costing you the job."

What ABOUT Asking, "What Are You Looking For?"

This is a real loaded question, because so often there really isn't a concise answer. There are a couple of reasons for this: First, even though the agency and director have given casting specs to the casting director, many times they won't know what they want until they actually see it living and breathing in front of them.

What's more, the information you receive can get lost in translation. Truth is, casting directors can't fully depend on agents to impart information to actors, because they rarely talk to the agents directly. One casting director described it this way: "I'll talk to some low-level assistant named 'Christy,' and she probably doesn't even know half the people she's talking to—if it's a casting director or the talent or whoever—and sometimes, Christy hands that information off to someone else who puts out the call to the actors. After a roundabout game of 'telephone' like that, it's amazing anybody even shows up in the correct wardrobe."

If there *is* an answer to, "What are you looking for?" The casting director should give you the low-down when you arrive. If not, go ahead and ask.

But what do you do when you *can't* find out what they are looking for?

One, believe that they're looking for *you.*

Two, you've really got to think about what it is that you can bring *to it.* The secret is not really to ask what it is they want, but to realize "how I can put myself *in* it."

And, most importantly, show them how right it would be to have you in it.

What to Ask at the Callback

The casting director should be an obvious presence at the callback, and there are a couple of crucial facts you should know. If the casting director isn't too harried, you should get an answer to these questions.

You might have gotten a clue from the date on the top of the script or the R2 or R3 next to it. Or there might be something about the copy that looks unfamiliar. In any case, it's okay to ask, "Has this copy changed?"

Commercials change all the time. Often, the agency goes to school on info gleaned from viewing the initial casting tapes, and if we find that a line or an action doesn't play, we'll rewrite it and bring the new idea to the callback. Frequently, the client may have had a hiccup over some piece of action, and that'll cause a rewrite. A hundred different events could spur script changes, and knowing this possibility gives you a legitimate reason to ask relevant questions about the concept or the part. ("This spot has changed. Is it still about the same thing?") Sometimes the casting director will even gather everybody around and impart a valuable tidbit, such as a line to be aware of or an approach to the scene. Listen up. This info may be coming from the director himself.

TIP: *Ask if the copy has changed.*

There's no harm in asking, "Am I still reading for the same part?" either. Roles get switched. Let's say you came in to read for the Husband, but the agency really thinks you're better for the Snoopy Neighbor. "Oh, gee, I didn't look at the neighbor; I looked at the husband!" Yikes!

Never assume!!

There may also be two scripts. Ask and they'll show you the right one.

Finally, ask if you're being paired with someone. If so, find someone to run lines with, even if you're not going to go in with them.

SOMETHING STINKS

You will encounter an amazing array of situations asking you to do mostly harmless, silly things. But let's face it—there are a lot of shitty TV spots out there that do degrading things to actors. Somewhere along the line you may step in one and have to make a decision whether you'd really want to do it if you indeed booked it. Are you desperate enough to work that you'd do something that's against your principles? Badly need the money? Well, gee, I hope you're not in that frame of mind, because all you end up doing is punching holes in your self-esteem.

I have a theory that the reason there are so many bad commercials on TV is that the scripts are bad to begin with, and only bad actors are willing to sacrifice their integrity to work in them.

When you really believe that something about a commercial stinks and your reputation could suffer (let alone the idea that living with it would give you the creeps), here's what to do:

Obviously a good time to time to say "no" is when the commercial is first described to you. Find a way to politely decline. But, of course, when "Christy" calls with information about the audition, she may not give you the real low-down; the spot may *sound* innocent and off you go to the initial call. Okay, at this time, if you look at the script and think, "This is terrible! I'm not going to do this!" then go to the casting assistant or casting director and politely tell them that you've just gotten a call from day care about your kid (or some plausible excuse) and that you're sorry but you can't audition. Don't tell them that the spot stinks! Just move on and call your agent or whoever got you into the call and explain the situation.

> **TIP:** *If you don't want to do it, politely refuse as early as you can.*

Now, if you're still uncertain about the script until you actually go in and read, be a pro and give it your best shot. At least you'll have confirmed your suspicions about the script, maybe performed well enough that you made a good impression, which could get you called for something else down the line, and had the valuable experience of another audition. Afterwards, call your agent or whoever got you into the call and tell him what's bugging you and that, if called back, you respectfully decline.

The worst thing an actor can do is turn down the spot after he or she gets cast. This causes huge problems and can put you out of favor for future projects, not only with the agency and the production company, but especially with the casting director.

Needless to say, an actor who develops cold feet on the shoot is going to find himself or herself in a really difficult situation. (Remember the guy opening the Christmas presents?) I've never experienced an ugly scene where an actor said he wouldn't perform something, but I have witnessed actors who could *barely* perform (in one case, ninety-five takes for a fifteen-second commercial!), and it's truly horrible to go through.

My dad was shot down over Germany in World War II. He said that the best thing to do in a situation like that was to bail out as early as possible. Good advice.

WAITING-AREA TIPS

Here's a bag of useful tips gathered from casting directors and veteran actors:

○ Find some place to read the copy out loud so that the first time it comes out of your mouth isn't when you're in the studio.

○ If you're going to go in to read soon, stand up. Stay on your feet so that you can maintain your energy.

○ When the part you're reading for is a large one, especially if it's a monologue, *don't waste your time trying to memorize the script*; there will be one hanging next to the camera on a cue card within your eye line (a union stipulation). Just get familiar with it. No one has ever gotten a part because someone in the back of the room observed, "Wow, that girl is a great memorizer!"

○ If you're paired with a kid, particularly at first call, find a good kid! And work with that kid. If they call you in with somebody else, say, "Oh, gee, can I go in with Timmy 'cause Timmy and I have been working on this and we're pretty good together." And the casting director will undoubtedly say, "Well sure, okay, since you've been working on it."

○ Are you a redhead? Then find a redheaded kid. Blonde? You got it.

- If you've chosen a kid who isn't that good, then get lost in the john for awhile and hope the munchkin gets swept in to read with somebody else.

- If you've been paired with someone bad, don't throw it all away and say, "Well I'm screwed, forget this." You act your little heart out. Don't give up because it'll be pretty apparent to everybody watching that "She's good, but that guy she's with stinks. Let's see what happens when we bring her back with somebody else." Sometimes you'll get a callback based on an observation like that, even when you *wouldn't* have gotten one if you were in with someone of equal talent.

- Carry a little emergency kit; things change. Say you arrive and you're suddenly reading for the Boss, instead of the Phone Installer. Well, guys, always have a jacket and a tie with you for times like these so you can switch wardrobe. Likewise, have a ball cap and a denim jacket available. Remember what we've previously discussed about wardrobe, though. And remember that your clothes should be one of your uniforms.

- If you live in a town where you mostly drive to calls, keep stuff in your car. If you ride a bus, subway, or train, travel light. For cripes sake, don't drag in a giant bag of clothes.

- Women should always have a little bag of accessories handy: a scarf or two to dress something up, extra earrings. And be prepared to do something with your hair; carry a scrunchie, tieback, or hairpins, because, invariably on a callback, somebody will want to see your hair different.

- Never bring props unless asked.

- If you wear glasses, *wear them*! Don't put your vanity before common sense. Actors who come in without their glasses on (or who didn't put in their contacts), who squint at the cue card, and fumble around are useless. Casting director Dorothy Kelly related an incident where an actor told her that the reason he hadn't worn his glasses was because his character in the storyboard didn't have glasses.

Jeesh! If you get the part, you'll use your glasses to memorize it, and then you'll go in front of the camera without them.

○ The character wears glasses and you don't? Maybe it would be a good idea to have an attractive-looking pair of nonprescription glasses in your emergency kit, eh?

○ You see the character in the storyboard doesn't look like you. Don't worry. There are a thousand reasons why, and none of them should concern you.

BEFORE GOING INTO THE STUDIO

This piece of advice applies especially to callbacks.

Please leave all of your bags, wardrobe, children, and what-have-you (except your purse, ladies, and something to tie back your hair) outside with the casting assistant. Bringing that stuff into the studio becomes baggage that you have to stash and attend to, and that takes precious time away from your main reason for being there: focusing on the work. What's more, it's a huge distraction to us.

Some actors think they've discovered this really cool trick of bringing stuff into the room. They use the time it takes to gather everything up as they're leaving as a device to buy more face time. They think, by staying in the room a tad longer, they'll be asked to read again. Well, as Rocky used to say to Bullwinkle, "That trick never works!" It doesn't buy anything but impatient looks from the crew in back of the room. It's annoying. What you *don't* want the agency to talk about after you've left is something like, "She was really good." "Yeah, but man was she annoying with all that crap she had with her." Now you've got a director thinking, "Uh-oh, high-maintenance actor."

TIP: *Leave your wardrobe and kids out in the lobby.*

ARE YOU READY? SOME WORDS FROM THE WISE

Okay, you've looked over the script and discovered what the concept is, you have a fair idea of how the spot's constructed, and you've found a line that's got the element of surprise to it. You've got a good idea about how this spot works. But before you make any final decisions about how you fit into this thing, take a few seconds to *visualize* the spot in your head. Watch it play on your mind's TV. Don't worry if your inner vision isn't how the spot will really be shot; the idea is to allow yourself to get into some kind of flow. And before you go in, don't forget—we want you to win.

> **TIP:** *Remember, we want every actor to win.*

Finally, here are some helpful thoughts from some successful commercial actors and casting directors:

"When you pick up the material, you must ask, what can I add to this to make them need *me? Why do they need me? . . . The most successful people in the business have this attitude: 'What can I bring to this?' Every script is a puzzle to solve, a game you can play to try to figure out what you can do with the material. The worse the commercial, the more work you should be doing to make it better."*

"Make yourself a team player. Right away, make yourself part of the creative process—which the casting session is. When you are in there with us, you're part of the team that's trying to make this thing sing. Make us feel that you want to help us.*"*

"I just know that every piece of copy is written for me. So in my mind, when I read the copy, I know that someone has me in mind for it. So the confidence level is pretty much there already. So I go in and think, 'This is what you wanted, right?'"

"I remember seeing Huey Lewis at Jazz Fest in New Orleans follow Fats Domino in concert. And he said something [to the audience] like, 'I was back there shaking, saying, "how can a guy like me follow Fats Domino?" Well folks, all I can do is play my tunes.'

"It's great to go to class. But a lot of actors will get in this class or that class and they'll develop the idea that, 'This is the way that you do it.' Like any other endeavor, like fixing your old Camaro, you get

as much information as you can and then you do what you think is best with what you have available. I worry that people think there's an absolute way of doing things. There's no such thing."

TIP: *Make us feel that you want to help us.*

OH, AND ONE LAST THING

TURN OFF YOUR DAMN CELL PHONE! Your phone rings during your audition, you die.

⑪ In the Studio

Master of mangled quotations, former Vice President Dan Quayle once said, "What a waste it is to lose one's mind. Or not to have a mind is being very wasteful. How true that is."

In his strange but prescient way, he pretty much described what happens at auditions.

Whether the agency and the director are reviewing first-call auditions on tape or sitting in the studio during callbacks, we're guaranteed to see at least one actor shoot him-or herself in the foot. The camera rolls and the actor is either trying too hard, trying to impress us, or just flat out doesn't know what to do.

Here's how to maintain your presence of mind when someone says "action."

MAKING CHOICES

Bernard Hiller advises, "A savvy actor is someone who comes into the room with an idea in mind. The commercial will give you ideas, but you should come up with some other ideas, as well, to show them, 'Hey, let's try it like this or like that.' I recommend that actors *not* do exactly what's there, but to do more. Give them more than they expect."

Whether you think it's the wrong one or the right one, come in with a choice. Even if it's wrong, you're better off than having no choice at all. Because if you make an *honest* mistake, your choice will at least give you an intelligent basis to ask a question or make an easier transition to the area the director wants you to occupy.

There's a big difference between making a wrong choice and a *bad* choice, however.

If you decide to make weird script interpretations or do something off the wall purely because you feel it'll make an impression, that's a bad choice. Make choices based on the truth you see in the script.

> **TIP:** *Coming in with a bizarre choice designed to make some sort of impression will only make a bad impression.*

And don't forget who you are. When the time comes for "action," please, don't read as a character if you *aren't* the character they describe. Moving out of your range or trying to be someone who's really different than you is fine in the greasepaint-flexing arena of a repertory theater, but it doesn't work very well here. It's just a bad choice. I'm always disappointed by this Jekyll and Hyde behavior, and it usually goes something like this:

We're casting for a "harried but likable waitress at a casual-dining family restaurant." She has two lines: "Are you ready to order?" and "How is everything?" An intriguing woman appears on tape and slates. She's the right type and something about her says she's waited tables before (maybe even this morning!). She speaks with no discernible accent. I like her. But right after "action," something strange happens. She chooses to become a wiseass, gum-cracking southern waitress, sort of like Flo from the seventies sitcom *Alice*. She even adds the word "honey'" to the end of the first line. Now, where did *that* come from? Okay, even though the part wasn't described as a "Flo," if she *honestly was* a Polly Holliday–type, we might be interested in calling her back to see what she could really do. But no, that interesting lady we saw a second before has disappeared, and was suddenly replaced by an actor who was ACTING. That wasn't her at all.

Why do actors make bad choices? Some honestly believe that they're bringing something extra to the part, but when they add another layer, which causes them to step away from their core capabilities, then they become the person we're not looking to cast. Some just don't do their homework. Others try to impress us with some perceived special ability (dialects are popular), and that makes us suspicious that they're covering up for a lack of ability.

SLATING

When you come in to any call, before you to start to act, the camera will focus on you, you'll be told that they've begun taping, and you'll be asked to say your name and (often) the name of whoever represents you. That's called the *slate*, and it's an old filmmaking term: Scene information was scrawled on a small slate that was held up in front of a camera before a scene was shot. (Nowadays they use a digital one called a "marker," sometimes referred to as "sticks.") Don't worry; nothing will be held up in front of the camera at an audition. They'll just say, "Tell us who you are, please." And you'll tell 'em.

At the first call you only have one shot at winning, and later, while we're reviewing auditions, your slate will be the first thing we see, the first impression we have of you. It'll show us how you react to the camera and deal with it when it focuses on you. Slates are especially revealing because we get a glimpse of people as they *really are* just by saying their names. It's amazing what shows just by saying your name on camera. What are you? Naturally serious and studious? Naturally bubbly and feminine? A natural exhibitionist? Whoever and whatever you are, a good rule of thumb is to *slate as yourself*, not *in character*.

> **TIP:** *Slate as yourself because good directors are always looking under the skin for the real person inside.*

For example, the casting specs say, "She sounds like Miss Piggy." Your agent calls you and asks, "Beth, can you sound like Miss Piggy?" "Moi?" you answer, "Of course." So you go to the first call and stand in front of the camera to slate. Now, even if you don't sound or look or have anything to do with Miss Piggy in real life, but you can *do* her, *don't* do her when you slate. On the other hand, if, in some way, you possess a Miss Piggy quality about you, or if you somehow sound like her naturally, then you can't help that when you slate as yourself you'll be Miss Piggy-ish. That's just you, but the point is, it's *really you*. That's what we want to see.

There's another angle. Say that the part you're reading for is some kind of a stereotypical, swaggering, mullet-haired Philadelphia punk, and that's the kind of person you are (Yo!)—you'd want to slate as yourself. But dig this—what if the part was for somebody like a butler, somebody against your type? Slating as your Philly self could open the director's mind to some really wacky possibilities. (Not to mention choosing to play the butler as yourself.)

Slate as yourself because good directors are always looking under the skin for the real person inside. According to director Danny Levinson, "If you slate your name and go into character they can see where you can go. If you're automatically the character they never know where you started."

Director Michael Norman has this surprising observation:

"It's good for them to slate as themselves. And if they're really good at *becoming* that character it's almost more impressive to see them *change* into that character.

"I think that if you're paying attention at all as a director—maybe even if they were off demographically for the part—I may think, 'Well they're wrong for this, but for this *other* spot I'm working on they'd be great.' And I can bring them in on that. So I think that [slating as yourself] can open the door for the director to think about you in a different way."

> **TIP:** *Don't slate as the character unless that character is really, really a part of your personality.*

Some fortunate people can naturally slate as a character, others rarely get away with it. Every so often, however, somebody will do something totally off the wall and make it happen.

I once saw a young guy belch his name—it was priceless, risky, but he made it work because he knew the part called for a young wiseass and he was a, well, a young wiseass. He couldn't help it. I also remember one time a very funny stand-up comic came in and did Sylvester Stallone as Rocky (and somebody else, I can't recall) for his slate. We ended up hiring him. Now, how did he get away with doing Rocky? Because he was good. *Really* good, and he knew it. And he subsequently demonstrated his talent with the way he handled the copy—sans Rocky.

How can some people come close to chewing up the scenery, yet make us embrace them? Mostly because they're not forcing it. Because that thing they do is an innate part of their personality and it's just *there*. It's part of their *it*. People with this brand of derring-do tend to be more relaxed than everybody else, and you can really see it. Their state of relaxation and being in the moment makes us believe that they're a person we can work with.

But unless you're really confident in yourself, beware, because clever ideas designed to make an impression on us can backfire:

Once, there was a guy who came in on a first call, and we saved his audition tape to show everybody just because his slate was so misguided. We were casting for a good-looking, normal, hunky-sorta guy. Up on the screen comes this really good-looking, normal guy. But, when asked to slate, instead of just being himself he struck this sort of ultra-cool pose, cocked his head with . . . this . . . like . . . *attitude* and said, "Hi, I'm Eddie So-and-So. *Babe Magnet!*" Now, I thought, well, he's nervous and he's trying to be cute or funny or different, okay fine, he didn't pull it off, and it was distracting. But the two female agency producers in the room saw this hunky guy say "Babe Magnet" and they both held their noses and said, "*eeew!*" Needless to say, they fast-forwarded the poor guy into oblivion. And unfortunately, those women would remember him if he showed up on a future session.

In fact, we used to have a special classification for actors like that: "Born to Be Fast-Forwarded." You don't want to be one of those actors.

> **TIP:** *If you think you have something shocking or clever up your sleeve, keep it there.*

As casting director Dorothy Kelly has said, "Slate as simply as if you're introducing yourself to someone new. Don't try to be funny on the slate, because unless you're Robin Williams, chances are you're not funny."

Bottom line: the camera comes on and you've gotta look like you're relaxed and ready to go to work. You've gotta be yourself, or you're never going to make it to the callback.

TIP: *The best rule of thumb: Slate as yourself.*

LEAVE THE SELLING TO US

Okay. This should be a no-brainer, but agencies see this happen way too often. It's the most misguided performance choice an actor can make, and that's when actors—usually new ones—try to *sell* what's being advertised in the commercial. Turning a line or lines, or a piece of business, into a statement that is overtly "selly" is the mark of an amateur.

TIP: *Don't overtly sell a product. Keep it real.*

Ads are ads. Selling is the purpose, yes, but except in the case of Anti-Ads, the ad agency has already woven sales info into the commercial, so *you don't have to be the salesperson.* Our job is to sell. Your job is to be real. (Besides, most of the time the VO handles the heavy lifting for the hard sell or product descriptions.) The last thing we want to see is someone selling something.

This usually happens with Spokesperson ads, Testimonials, and Problem/Solution ads because they're the ones most likely to contain a few lines of hard-sell copy, such as:

"I can see my face in it!"

Or,

"The solution to our debt problems was a Loan-Co solution."

And so on.

Unless directed otherwise, please resist the temptation to hammer on lines like these. Start from a real place and you'll be better off in your audition, because even if you're asked to stink up the place like a local car-dealer spokesperson, you'll still be based in your own reality.

As one veteran director observes, "I really like subtle acting—even in commercials—that more approaches movie acting. So this is something that makes me personally mad: When I see an actor come in and assume that in a commercial they need to overact. I'm insulted by that. Not that I would treat them ugly, but I would write them off for that, right off the bat. . . . [Especially] if I've said after they did a take, 'You can throw it away more. Make it feel more off the cuff. You don't need to hit the product line like that.' . . . People that assume that they should overact, well, I feel like I'm being talked down to as a director, because they feel that commercials are all about bad acting."

Now, if you think you could have (or do have) trouble delivering phony-sounding sales dialogue—especially out-and-out sales copy like, "It's got the biggest payload in its class!" or, "Buy two and get the third one free!"—then get thee to a commercial acting class and work on getting comfy with ad copy. Funny as it sounds, you need to find a way to make lines like those believable.

Same goes for action and business. Unless somebody tells you differently, don't go ape-shit over the remarkable "new-car-finish" wax job on the junky old Ford Fiesta, or the spicy taste of Buffalo Bob's Bob-A-Q Sauce. We won't buy it and neither will the average TV consumer. It just looks fake.

MESSIN' WITH THE SCRIPT

A major mistake that some actors make is that they somehow feel that they need to rewrite the words or change a piece of designated action. We've had people ask, "Uh, are you guys married to the concept?" Well, gee, let's think about that for a moment. Mmmm. Why, by golly, no! Are you a copywriter? Wow, really? Yeah go ahead!

Jeez.

Intentionally rewriting our precious script is like writing your own death certificate. Unless you've been specifically asked to improvise an entire scene, please, do not *intentionally* change lines or add new words because you think it's going to enhance the spot or your performance. It won't, for two good reasons.

Number one: Our old nemesis, Time. You've seen storyboards now. You've seen how action and words fit together in a constrained environment. Every shot has been carefully timed out. Everything said and seen has been timed out to the nanosecond. So if you start adding time to the spot because you think you have a better idea for the script, you won't make it beyond the first call, and being clever in the callback will definitely be detrimental. If you do it in the room, the director will believe you'll do it on the shoot. So, when you have extracurricular ideas for the script, use them as subtext.

TIP: *Never intentionally change the script unless asked.*

Reason number two: You can really piss people off. You're aware, now, of how much effort goes into creating and writing a commercial. And you remember our god, the Client? Well he's made a whole lotta agency people sweat blood over those words you're reading. Entire ad agency creative departments have had their butts kicked just to make sure that the ad is conveying exactly what the client wants to say. He's probably stepped on one little sentence in that script ten times already. So don't purposely mess with the words. The agency will have a cow.

Oh, sure, there are a few actors that get hired because they can intentionally bend a script into a unique performance. Yeah, they mess with the words, but we know that's what they do and they're good at it, and that's why they're called in. They're there because that's what they do.

Remember, there's a difference between messing around with a script and using improv to get yourself out of a jam. If you blow a line in a dialogue scene, improv can help you keep the action going. An actor who has the ability to keep all the balls in the air shows us something important: Resilience.

WHEN THINGS GO WRONG

"But what if I blow a line or get lost!?" you ask. "That adds time." Yes it does, but this is an audition and we don't expect you to perform everything exactly right in thirty seconds, and neither should you. Obviously, at a first call or even a callback, you'll be in unfamiliar territory. Naturally, words get bobbled or a script can take longer to perform—that's bound to happen. So don't put a lot of pressure on yourself by trying to do *everything* right. You can't. You'll make yourself crazy. Nonetheless, if we see you *consciously adding stuff* to the commercial, we'll suspect that you'll do that when the camera is really rolling and the meter's running. And, as you can imagine, that's not a good thing.

> **TIP:** *We don't expect you to get everything* exactly *right in a first read.*

Actor Kevin John Reilly has been in the business since 1984, and he remembers an audition where he only had one line—and blew it.

"I had an audition for Burger King. They were looking for fireman types. And the copy was, 'Hot roast beef melted cheese real hot.' Now, a lot of times when you go in they'll have the words up there on the board where you can read it and not worry about memorizing it. But it was so easy—you know, just hot roast beef melted cheese real hot—it's not rocket science, so there wasn't a board up there. We were going in four at a time and I was the first one to audition, and I start off with 'hot roast beef melted cheese . . .' and the brain left me. Couldn't think of the rest of it. So I basically did one of those little 'David Lettermans'—you know, where he turns his head like a dog going, 'What are you up to?'—and I looked right in the camera and said, 'You know there's so much damn copy I'll have to read it again. Excuse me one second.' And I didn't do it in a mean way or a hurtful way. It's just that you've got to have fun. When I blew the line . . . well, it's like I already figured it was done so just do something goofy and have fun with it. So I ran to the side, and the camera is still running and they can hear me going, 'Oh, this copy,' and saying silly stuff. Then I jumped back in and delivered 'Hot roast beef melted cheese real hot.'

"Next day I get a callback. And for forty-five minutes they had me say that line every which way that I could until I was getting loopy. And afterwards I just didn't feel like I nailed it or not. But I got a call and I'm booked! And I ended up doing three of them.

"I think that moment where I went off, that's probably what got me the job, because I relaxed, I had fun with it. I think the director could see, 'Oh, he had fun with it, didn't get flustered, took a negative and made it into a positive.'"

Okay, what happens if you get lost in a monologue, or a dialogue scene, and your scene partner has a brain fart? Should you stop midstream and ask to start over? The best advice is to keep going. Your job is to show everybody, "Hey, I don't have any problem here." Often I've seen two actors blow a line, stay true to the action with improv, and make us smile in the process. They stayed cool and poised, and we were impressed by their ability to hang tough.

> **TIP:** *If something throws you off track, try to keep going.*

When you blow a line, or get lost or bobble a prop and you have the presence of mind to keep on going, after you finish it would be appropriate to say, "I know I screwed that line up there," or, "Obviously I klutzed that prop, so would it be all right if I gave it another shot?" The director knows what happened and should give you another chance—but, just to keep you on your toes, probably with different direction.

Just like in any stage play, *things outside of your control* are bound to go wrong at a callback. You're in a brightly lit room full of strangers. Phones ring just as you're starting to act. People enter the room unexpectedly. The video recorder runs out of tape halfway through your take. Props *never* work. And sometimes, unavoidably, the whole thing has to stop. Okay, stay cool. Most of the time whatever caused the work stoppage will be pretty obvious to everyone, and you can say something very professional, like, "Hey, can we reload this thing?" And you'll get another chance. But don't get annoyed. No, no, no. Blow it off. Take a deep breath. Make a joke about it and move on. Even if you're really pissed about being interrupted, don't show it. Ever. Because if you do, then the director will feel that on the shoot, which is infinitely more chaotic than an audition, you won't be able to handle it.

There are poltergeists in the room, and they're going to spring out of hiding at any moment. Half the battle comes from *knowing* things can go wrong, which makes it that much easier for you to deal with when they do. Expect them and you'll be able to keep your composure. If possible, you may even be able to use an interruption or a bad prop to your advantage. Your ability to roll with the punches is crucial because, likewise, if the director sees an actor *panic* in an uncomfortable situation, then he knows the actor's going to panic on the set. And, like I've said before, one of the main reasons the same actors get hired over and over is because they're cool and flexible; i.e., they're reliable.

> **TIP :** *If something goes wrong, never, ever let on that you're upset about it.*

Let's say your audition was wrinkle-free but you simply felt you could perform it better. Can you ask to read, "One more time, please?" That depends. At the initial call you may be working in a more sympathetic atmosphere and you'll get your chance. You might even be asked to do it again without prompting. At a callback where the director likes you, you could be asked to read it again, but this time the director will probably give you a new choice to see how you handle his curveball. But before you pop the question, pause for a moment and listen to the feel of the room. You should be able to gauge the acceptance of your performance by the vibe, and the director's body language, and the look on his or her face. Go? No go? Even if it looks like go and you ask to do the piece again, be prepared to be turned down and accept it graciously. Live to fight another day. (In chapter 13 we'll explore in detail the questions you can ask a director.)

> **TIP :** *Be prepared: If you ask to read it again you'll probably get turned down.*

IMPROVE WITH IMPROV

I encourage every actor to take improvisation classes. Improv teaches you how to work naked with nothing more than an idea to play off. You survive by your wits without the security blanket of a script. This is scary. But the challenge is really worth it because improvisation techniques will force you to use your head, and condition you to embrace those moments when the train goes careening off the rails. You'll have an advantage over everybody else because you'll know that when something goes wrong, it's *real*. Real is where it all comes alive. It is all about being.

One of the basic rules of improv is that every question is answered in the positive. This keeps the action moving forward. For example, let's imagine you were improvising a scene that took place at a bowling alley and you asked your scene partner, "Gee, are these lanes made out of Teflon?" If she answered "no," you can see that the action wouldn't have any place to go and you'd be standing there with flop sweat breaking out on your forehead. But if she said something in the positive, like, "Wow, you could almost skate on them!" then the action can move forward. This simple rule forces you to stay in the moment. Consequently, if the bottom ever drops out in an audition, you'll feel comfortable because you'll know how to stay in the moment. You won't be scared.

WORKING WITH THE CAMERA

More often than not, you'll be auditioning in front of a locked-down video camera. "Locked-down" means that the camera sits on a tripod and doesn't physically move around. (Tracking or handheld camera work at auditions is pretty rare.) For the sake of keeping things simple, the camera generally sits in the same place, shooting from the same angle all day. Often the camera operator will zoom in or zoom out to simulate camera work that may happen during actual filming, but that's about it for tricky camera moves. Note that even though you may gather from the storyboard that they'll be shooting from many angles when the commercial is finally filmed, don't worry about that here.

If you happen to be reading a monologue or extended copy, there's a cool way to take advantage of a locked-down camera: If the camera is squarely in front of you while you sit or stand on your mark, never face the camera directly, *or* perform in profile—unless you are specifically asked to. You're going to look much better if you angle your body three quarters to the camera while standing or sitting, or when playing a static scene with another actor. Sitting or standing three quarters to the camera makes for a prettier, more dynamic line because it allows your head to face toward the camera while slightly opening up your shoulders and torso. You'll look more at ease, especially when the camera is directly in front of you. It's a simple thing to do, and you can try this in a full-length mirror at home: Stand facing the mirror with your head and body parallel to the mirror and pretend the camera is directly in front of you. Take your left foot back about half a step or so and allow your body and shoulders to turn naturally out with the step. Your head's still facing the camera, but notice how your right shoulder has crept in a touch, causing you to look as if you've turned your head, even when you haven't. Now try it with your right foot going back. Same result. Subtle, yes, but effective.

> **TIP:** *Don't face the camera squarely or perform in profile unless asked to.*

When you're sitting or standing center stage and the camera's down-right, don't square up to the camera. Cheat your body to your right so that your left shoulder is slightly closer to the camera angle, and turn your head to face the camera. When the camera's down left, cheat your body to your left so that your right shoulder is slightly closer to the camera angle and turn your head to face the camera. Practice this a couple of times at home and you won't forget.

If you find yourself in the classic situation of holding a product up somewhere near your face, you'll more than likely be shot square to the camera. This angle is used simply to allow for maximum product star focus. If you hold the product in your right hand, cheat your left shoulder back and you'll accomplish two things: You'll reveal more of the left side of your face for our viewing pleasure. And you'll give the product a slight nudge forward toward the camera.

Here are a couple of other camera-friendly suggestions:

When you're in a scene with other actors and you're all moving around, be aware of where the camera is, and for God's sake, don't turn your back on it.

The fourth wall applies here, too, so unless the script asks for action directly to the camera, don't look at it! Peeking at the camera is like wearing a flashing neon sign around your neck that says, "Hi, I'm an amateur!" and makes you a Born to Be Fast-Forwarded candidate.

Commercial audition classes should teach you to be aware of your framing. As you've learned, you could be framed in a tight close-up, close-up, from the chest up, medium shot, or wide, depending on the action.

If you've had the opportunity to look at a storyboard out in the lobby, you may discover that your character is being shot only in a close-up, and you can pretty much assume that your movement will be restricted. You may see that you're only in a wide shot, where you'll have more freedom.

But, you may see that you appear in a variety of shots. Or, more often than not, you'll only have a script to work from, and they rarely indicate framing. However, with a script, you *should* be able to judge your overall framing from the scene. For instance, if the scene has you snuggling with a baby, it's safe to play it as a medium close-up. In any case where your framing isn't so obvious, but you think it's important to know, go ahead and ask.

Director Nicholas Barker observes, "There are occasions—if it is a comedy scene—it's entirely legitimate for an actor to say, 'Am I acting in a wide shot, or am I acting in a close-up?' as long as the question is not motivated by egotism. You're just quietly and thoughtfully trying to communicate with the director so you've got the information to [be able to] give him or her what they need."

When it comes time to work on the set, Nicholas goes on to say, "It helps if an actor understands what a close-up is supposed to do and what a wide shot is supposed to do. I, for example, do a lot of 'observational' comedy, so I often shoot wide. So what I'll be looking for is the *signature* of somebody's movement and their ability to produce something that looks like choreography. What I'm noticing is how their personality and thought process and intention is expressed through the totality of their movement. In other words, I can't rely on the close-up to give me any information about what they are doing or thinking."

Occasionally at an audition, the director may ask for a zoom in or out, and you should be aware of those, too. Obviously, if the shot starts out very tight, you won't be able to move much until they go wider. Conversely, you'll have to allow your movements to become more still as the shot pushes in. In those cases you should be told how you're framed.

You need to stay real about all of this framing business, too. This is still the audition, not the shoot. Unless someone specifically gives you framing info up front, or you've dug it out of the script or board, don't peg your entire performance on whether you're framed tight or wide. Don't get all crazy about it. Getting hung up on the imaginary box you're working inside of is just another thing that can distract you from focusing on who you are in the commercial.

> **TIP:** *Unless it's really crucial to the scene, don't get hung up on how the camera is framing you.*

Often you'll be reading for a part that requires you to talk directly to the camera, and I can sympathize with actors who have problems with that. One of my bugaboos was being intimidated by the lens. I was never comfortable because it wasn't like playing a scene with other actors. Every time I was confronted by this eye staring back at me, I got uptight. (Imagine what I was like just doing my *slate*!)

If this is you, then you have some serious work to do to get over your intimidation, and the best place to accomplish that is in a class. The coach will have a lot of good exercises you can use, but here's one you may want to employ. Brian Gibson was an excellent "actor's director," and one of his tricks was to ask actors to turn the camera into a real person that they knew. Try it. Personalizing or visualizing can have a grounding effect, making your performance more intimate and real.

WORKING WITH PROPS AND PRETENDING

Production companies hire hand models for all the intricate, close-up stuff like turning on switches, chopping vegetables, picking up and displaying small items and so on, so don't get too hung up about actually doing such tasks. However, you are going to find yourself in situations where the script calls for you to bite into a sandwich, or stock some shelves, or drive a car, or assemble a bicycle, or drink a beverage, or perform any of a million everyday tasks that put you in touch with an object or environment.

There may be actual props for you to handle in the studio or stand-ins for you to use. Very often, there won't be anything in the room because—let's use a car for example—they're not going to pull in a new Taurus for everybody to sit in. More than likely, you'll sit on a folding chair, working with thin air.

When you sit down in the imaginary car, I have only one thing to say: Keep it real, AND DON'T OVERDO IT!!!

Are you a mime? Probably not, but if you are I apologize because I don't like mimes at commercial auditions unless the spot calls for one. Listen, if you get the part you'll be strapped into a real Taurus. We don't need to see your arm draped out the window of an imaginary car door while you adjust the seat, pop in a CD and fiddle with buttons that aren't there! Save the mime stuff for the Street Faire.

Keep the action simple.

Testimonials seem to bring out nervous behavior in actors. Michael Norman says, "One bit of advice about testimonials in a callback: avoid the trap of too much busy work. Those kind of spots work if [the acting] is based on a certain confidentiality, charisma, 'off-the-cuffness,' or informality. Actors tend to want to pick up props and walk and talk and do things like that, and I think you're better off not marching around, but sitting calmly and not being so authoritative. By being low-key—more like you're talking to a friend—that's what makes those scripts feel better. You come off more confident about the product that way. . . . Less is more."

> **TIP**: *Props and action: The simpler, the better.*

Now, with food or beverages, it can get a little hairy. There's usually a piece of bread or some crackers or a glass of water on the table to represent the real thing, and you'll be judged on how realistically you bite or how you sip these rudimentary props. No kidding. Some actors can't seem to eat or drink without making it look phony. You must find a way to make it real. Even if you give a knockout performance, if you can't realistically bite into a piece of stale bread at the audition, how can we expect you to bite into our client's Macho Burrito on camera?

The toughest thing to do is hold up a tube of toothpaste or a jar of active hydrating beauty fluid in an unnatural position next to your face, talk about it, and make it look like you do this kind of thing every day. Can you? It's a mysterious feat that can't be explained in any book, so you'll need your commercial acting coach to work with you to make the unnatural become natural. She'll show you how to embody objects with friendly powers.

> **TIP**: *Work on props in class, not in your audition.*

⑫ Back at the Agency

Looking at First-Call Auditions: How We Choose
Who Makes the Cut

To the uninitiated, an agency first-call reviewing session can be a daunting experience. The creative team and the producer all sit in a room at the office zooming through tapes of audition after audition, giving thumbs-up and thumbs-down and reviewing performances with language that sounds like a cross between Roger Ebert and Andrew Dice Clay.

Somewhere off campus, the director is reviewing tape, as well. He'll usually check off five to seven actors he likes for each part, the agency will make choices, too, and we'll compare notes. You'll find that some of the better directors have worked with certain actors, and they'll alert us to watch out for somebody they like. "Hey, keep an eye out for so-and-so. I worked with her and she's really good." An endorsement like that can color our opinion in such a way that even though this anointed talent didn't really perform well, the director will make us feel that, "Look, even if you didn't see it today, this girl's gonna do better than anybody else we saw." In a case like that, it's a lock that that actor is going to be called back—even if she doesn't look right for the part.

Director Michael Norman says, "I really watch casting tapes intently. I watch casting tapes *at least* twice. I'll kind of breeze through them and get the lay of the land and make sure everything is going okay and good people are showing up. And I'll question—I never mark people, I'll just [internally] question them—and then I'll go back through again, right before the callback, and in a disciplined way look at who's interesting. I'll skip over people who, for whatever reason, are just *so* demographically wrong and maybe weren't interesting in the first run-through. I won't take the time to look at those, but everybody I've questioned I'll look at very intently. That way I'll really know what they're doing, and I'm not going to want to change them to a different person when they come into the callback.

"I'm surprised that people who I've thought were just wonderful on the initial casting tape [finally] get in the room with all the people and they're just flat. There's nothing there. That happens sometimes. And sometimes there's the phenomenon where someone's great at the callback, and you get 'em at the shoot and they're phhttt. It's rare, but I've had that happen where they're, ah, underwhelming."

Depending on the commercial, there may be a couple hundred actors to review. That's a lot of people to evaluate in a half day, and man oh man, it makes for a very wacko situation. One after another, actors pop up on screen saying the same lines. Occasionally someone will have something good going on and we'll play her audition over a couple of times. "Yes? No? Okay, call her back." Sometimes someone appears and is such a hit we won't even play her back. She's in. But often someone appears whose look is so completely off base, or worse, he's obviously such a bad actor, that *zoom!* that actor barely gets his slate finished or says two words before he's . . . Yes. Born to Be Fast-Forwarded.

Okay, okay—now you think agency people are a bunch of cruel jerks. But here's the deal: We don't have the time to sit around and watch people who aren't right for the part or don't have their shit together. They get zapped because, for the most part, they deserve it. For sure, many actors come on screen who are really good, but they're just not right for the part or it "just isn't their script." We'll surely see them again sometime.

The bottom line is that you've got to make a strong, positive impression on that tape.

Don't forget *we want you to get the part.* You! We're pulling for you. We want our TV spot to be a success. We don't want to fail; therefore, we don't want *you* to fail.

When we look at tapes, we're always thinking, "The next person is going to be the one." Please be the one.

OUR CRITERIA

So, how do we decide if you get called back or get fast forwarded? Here are the criteria that I use, and that the producers, directors, and creative directors and teams that I respect use as well.

You Have to Be Right for the Part

Casting directors will always send their best choices of types based on our specs. Still, if you come in and we have a definite idea for the part and you ain't it, hey, that's no skin off your nose. Better luck next time. However, casting directors will often let us know they've auditioned a few actors who are against type, and they'll bring in some off-the-wall people. Every once in awhile someone will show up who makes us go, "Hey, we didn't think of *that* kind of person!" And sometimes the actor will get called back.

But, yes, sometimes an actor will be wrong for a part, yet they'll get called back. Sounds crazy, but some directors are crazy like a fox. Director Michael Norman's little trick is one more reason for you to keep an open mind when you're at the callback, but you realize you don't seem to fit:

"Something I tend to do is, I may see somebody on an initial tape and I'll think, 'They're totally wrong for this, but they're an interesting character and a good actor.' And I'll bring them to the callback just because I want to *meet* them. And I'll want to get their Polaroid and save it for something else, 'cause I think they're interesting and I've never seen 'em before.

"An actor may come in and feel like, 'Why did they call me back for this? My agent sends me and I'm totally wrong and I don't get it.' Well, it may be that the director is interested in you for something you never even thought of."

> **TIP:** *You could get called back to read for a part you're wrong for, because the director wants to keep you in mind for the future.*

You Must Be Believable

We have to believe that you are *being* that person in the commercial. As I laid down at the very beginning of the book, we don't want to see any "acting." And, as I've discussed, we want to see *you*.

When Danny Levinson looks at auditioners, he's impressed by people who are genuine. "You're looking for personality, but you're looking for *their* personality. First and foremost, I want to know that you're intelligent, that you understand what we're doing. And to be yourself. It's a weird thing; to act, you have to take on all these different personas, and in features and stuff, that's true. But commercials are a little different. Commercials are certainly about first impressions, both from my point of view and from the viewer's point of view. So the story is told when I first see you: I'll decide if I like you or dislike you."

Nicholas Barker adds, "When I'm casting, what I'm looking for, well, a number of things: First of all, I need to see whether or not the actor is in real life the character that he's playing. The truth of the matter is that most actors can only play one part. Occasionally, great technicians can play maybe two or three roles. But most people actually spend most of their careers being cast in one role. And it's good to know in advance what that role is, and how you can finesse it and tweak it so you can morph into similar roles, which are adjacent to the role in question.

"So the first thing that I as the director am looking for is, 'Does this person look, breathe, act like the character that I'm trying to cast?' If they're not, 'Do they have the intelligence to invent something that approximates what I have in mind?' When it comes to acting, there is no substitute for intelligence. The best actors I've worked with have either been highly intelligent, or they simply *are* the character that I'm looking for—in which case they don't have to be intelligent, but they do have to be reasonably good at taking direction."

You Can't Fake It

If there are physical requirements to the part, you must be able to handle them without question. Don't come into an audition if you really can't tap-dance or climb a rock wall. If you aren't really British, don't try out your veddy bad English dialect on us.

No Shtick

You may look right for the part, but if you come in unprepared or nervous or unfocused or just plain green and try to cover it up by doing shtick, then fuhgeddaboudit! You'd be amazed how many people retreat into a comfortable character or rely on familiar mannerisms to cover up their lack of ability. Battle-tested agency producer Michael Waters observes, "About the twentieth time you've seen somebody do Jack Nicholson, you don't care anymore." They are Born to Be. . . . Which leads to the next criterion.

We Must Be Convinced That You Are Completely Reliable

Those who listen and stay cool and flexible are more likely to make it to the callback. That's why if you screw around or talk a lot, don't listen to direction, rely on shtick, or deliberately rewrite the script, we won't feel that we can depend on you to concentrate and deliver a performance next Tuesday afternoon when the camera is rolling and we've only got a half hour of daylight left.

We Must Trust That You Are a Professional

Talent who appear on the initial call tape who are prepared and ready to go to work are the people who stand out from the crowd. There's an air about true professionals—they seem to be in complete control, yet so loose at the same time. It's immediately apparent that they've done their homework and that they're comfortable in the situation. When we see that, *our* comfort level instantly moves into the warm zone.

The best example of an actor who is *the* total professional is Hector Elizondo. In addition to his many fine screen and TV performances, he's also a first-rate voice-over talent. For a long time he was the voice for a popular restaurant chain, and I had the great good luck to direct him in countless radio and TV voice-over sessions. When Hector arrived, he always carried this air about him that made you feel like he was really happy to be there. He'd get in the booth, and bam—he was on. Kept his motor running, kept things light, but all business. And he was *so* good—this is voice-over, mind you, where time is crucial—that if you asked him to give you another read, but this time two-tenths of a second faster, he'd do it to the decimal point with exactly the same inflection! The man is the poster child for professional actors.

You Must Be Directable

The director has to feel strongly that you are an actor that he can easily work with. You may come in and be amazingly talented and special, but if the director sees that you can't listen, or thinks that you might be headstrong or a prima donna when you get on the set, then he may have second thoughts. Directors have a sixth sense for this. First call is a pressure situation, and they watch the tape to see how you handle it. If they don't sniff it out then, they definitely find out at the callback when you're both together.

The X-Factor

Maybe you don't look quite right, but you're the only one who got the line that everybody else has blown. We'll call you back. Maybe you don't look quite right, but there's something about you in particular, a quality that may change our thinking about the character. Is there potential there? Something that adds another dimension we hadn't thought of? That's the X-Factor and it goes hand in hand with the last criterion:

Perfection

Many actors over-rehearse. They think that what we're going for is perfection, but striving for perfection generally leads to a canned performance, which is the worst kind of acting. Actors who strive to find reality, with all the little imperfections and unexpected little nuances that make performances real, are the ones who get the job. The people who can inhabit the character *without becoming a tomato* will get hired. Try to find a way to be loose and spontaneous, because that's when you really create a character—not when you read that script perfectly.

I put this question to Howie Cohen, and his answer echoes those of other agency people.

QUESTION: Let's say seventy-five actors are up for a single role and you're viewing the tape from the initial call. What are the things an actor does that make you stop and watch him?

"Well, I don't particularly respond well to an actor coming in and trying to grab my attention—to get me to take note of this person just because they want me to remember *them*, as opposed to remembering what they did.

"The process I go through . . . well, a lot of it is very instant. It's based on a feeling I have about what I think this person looks like or should look like, or some kind of chemistry thing that happens when the tape comes on. And I can usually tell instantly with a lot of people that it's just not right. When I was younger, I'd watch the whole take before I would say, 'Mmm don't think so.' As I've gotten, *hopefully*, more professional and not just jaded, now sometimes I can say 'no' within the first ten seconds.

". . . That's what we try to look for when we're casting. Somebody who can be real, and if we think they can be real, then it's our job to try and find the way to make them most real when we're shooting.

"The idea of reality goes all the way back to the Alka-Seltzer 'I can't believe I ate the whole thing' spot. [A Clio classic.] It was all about isolating one moment. And I can still remember—even though it was pretty early on in my career, we thought it was a pretty funny script—I remember we saw so many people for that and how many wrong ways actors could say that line. But he [actor Milt Moss] sort of captured what me and my partner had in mind, and then he went well beyond what we envisioned it could be. And that really defines where I come from on just about anything I've done. To try to get as close to that moment of reality, because that's what's so touching. Those spontaneous moments of reality."

⓭ You've Made It to the Callback

Making the cut is quite an achievement. Think of it. You've impressed a director and the ad agency *from long distance*. They've only seen you on tape! Now's your chance to show them what you can do in person.

Previously, in chapters 10 and 11, you were given the golden keys to auditioning: how to slate; why you shouldn't rewrite scripts; how to pick a good kid to work with; how to work with a camera; how to keep going when you screw up; and so on. All of that knowledge is doubly useful at the callback because this time, it's for all the marbles. Use everything. I mean it.

Oh. They've called your name. It's showtime.

DOES IT MAKE A DIFFERENCE WHAT TIME YOU AUDITION?

Actors get concerned about the time that they're scheduled to audition during the course of the day. "Is it better to be there early in the process? At the end? What if the agency's already made a decision and they're just going through the motions?"

Because you don't have any control over the timing of your call, you shouldn't let it be a huge concern for you. Do everything you normally do to prepare.

However, there are two situations to consider. First, if you read early in the session, everybody in the room is fresh and more alert. What's more, actors that do a great job set a standard for everyone else to beat.

But if the callbacks are held in the afternoon or early evening and begin to run late, then you can probably expect more tension in the room, especially if you're going in near the very end of the session. The reason is simple. We're getting tired back there. We've probably already done a morning's worth of business at the agency, or in many cases, been traveling from New York, Chicago, or L.A. We've already seen a lot of people in a hot, stuffy little room, and still have a lot to do after you leave. So if there's a time to resist getting sucked into any downer atmosphere emanating from back there, I'd say it's late in the day. More than any other time, it's your job as a professional to make everyone feel at ease.

However, even though it's late, the good directors don't go to sleep. They're being paid an outrageous amount of money to make decisions, and most are more than aware of the value of their craftsmanship. Surely by then we'll have some actors sitting on that short pile of headshots known as the good stack, and our attention is starting to drift, but a good director will always be looking for somebody better. And hey, we could be in a situation where we haven't found anybody yet. You could come in at the eleventh hour and save our butts. I've seen it happen.

IT'S THE BIG ONE

The casting director ushers you into the studio and announces your name. It's bright, close, and sweaty in there. It reeks of Chinese takeout. You smile. You look around.

Everybody in the back of the room is talking. Who's back there? The agency writer and art director, possibly the creative director, the agency producer, people from the production company, including their producer, and of course, the director.

With the shoot only days away, production people are running in and out of the room to see the director. The set designer may show up with a bunch of sketches to approve. Other production people such as the art director, stylist, or director of photography may be hammering out last-minute shoot details with the director. Sometimes, the Almighty Client is back there breathing down our necks.

Everybody's on cell phones. They're eating M&M's and sipping decaf grandé nonfat extra hot lattes.

They're ignoring you.

"Hey!," you think, "It's me! . . . Hey! Helloooo! What's going on here? Isn't this an audition?"

Yes.

What Do You Do?

One day you could walk into a room as chaotic as a rush-hour subway station. Or you could be ushered into a gloomy funeral parlor and be met with a stony wall of silence—and believe me, that's *really* weird. Ya never know. Often someone new to all this will enter and suddenly resemble a nun who's somehow stumbled onto a porno shoot.

To quote Ralph Kramden: "Homina-homina-homina."

So what do you do? How do you react? How do you focus?

No matter what, try not to pick up on the energy of the room. Even if it appears that we're dealing with some kind of bad mojo, don't play into it. If you get a negative vibe pulsating from the back, that's just us. *It doesn't have anything to do with you.*

> **TIP:** *No matter what, try not to pick up on the energy of the room.*

Bernard Hiller recommends doing this: "When you walk in, you're not walking in to audition. *See yourself as going into the shoot.* It's a different attitude. You're not trying out anything. You're *there* already. You're part of the team, so you're going in to meet people who are already crazy about you. And even if they look really serious, that's how people look when they're really crazy about you."

The first thing to do is check out the space. After all, you've been trained to take a bare stage and turn it into an environment. So, take a quick moment to get a feel for the room and check out the area where you're going to be working. It could just be a chair or a bench. There could be a table in front of you with props on it. Go there and take focus. There may be nothing there at all. If that's the case, take a look on the floor to see if there's a mark for you to stand behind. No mark? Ten marks? Then see where the camera is pointing and put yourself in range. And take focus. When you don't know where to stand, ask! "Where would you like me to stand?" One of the benefits of asking is that you'll immediately make a connection with the director. He or she will generally be the first person to answer your question. And away you go.

TIP: *Forget about all those other people in the room. Take focus and seek the director's attention.*

Here's something that may not work for you, but it has for Troy Evans. "I always compliment them on the script—not in any great detail—but, well, I figure it's like going backstage at a play, right? If you can't find something nice to say to your friends, why the f**k are you going backstage? You know, if you're just going to go back there and say, 'Yeah, uh, wanna go get a burger?' Come on. They've been sweatin' for you for over two hours! I don't care if you hate the play, you go back there and you say, 'Wow, you were really great.' How does that hurt anybody? So it's the same thing. If I can't muster up some modest compliment for this script, why am I auditioning for it? It's just something to say instead of just going in and standing [around]. If you say, 'You know, this is a cute script. I like this,' it sort of breaks the ice and they'll say, 'Do you want to take a pass at it?'"

Come in with your choice. Come in ready to work. And if you're thrown by all the chaos (or the silence, or the overpowering smell of moldering Kung Pow), if you've done all your preparation you'll at least *look* like you're ready to work. That's the quality that always amazes me about the true professionals. They just plain give you the impression that they're ready to work, and by doing so, make all of us people sitting back here in Decision Land feel a lot more comfortable.

TIP: *Actors who at least* look *like they're ready to work put us at ease.*

I've said this before: Remember that we're all pulling for you. We want you to win. To us, every actor who walks through that door is the person we want in our commercial. After all, if we don't cast the spot, we are screwed. So, even though it may seem that we're out of sorts, or even rude at times, deep down inside we're on your side. The only person who's not going to give you the job is you.

Auditions are never perfect. But commercial auditions are more never perfect than the rest. Expect anything, and you'll be better prepared to deal with everything.

> **TIP:** *When you come into the studio think of yourself entering a cocktail party that's already going full tilt. Everybody isn't necessarily going to stop talking and drinking because you've arrived. When the spotlight finally falls on you, then it'll be your chance to be wonderful.*

Here's what some very seasoned directors say about what your entrance says about you:

". . . everybody appreciates somebody that comes in that's very composed and they aren't too big of a personality. Some people come in and think, 'maybe if I go to the back of the room and grab some M&M's or say hi to everybody in the room, they'll *remember* me.' Part of it may be that, but part of it may be that they're naturally gregarious. Whichever way you are, I think it's good to come in receptive and friendly, but respecting that these people in the room are going to be in there all day long looking at thirty or more people doing exactly the same script. You want somebody that respects that process and doesn't create a lot of disturbances.

"You want to see, I guess, a calm friendliness. The first thing that you want to get from the actor is, 'would you want to be on a set with this person?' So you want them to be pleasant, alert, and listening—listening to hear your—the director's—story. You give them valuable information when they come in, and I make a point—I think there are a lot of directors who are different [than me], who don't introduce themselves to every actor. They let the casting director bring actors into the room and tell 'em what to do and they just watch—and so I always make a point of walking up and introducing myself to them and making some kind of personal contact, which I think gives them permission or frees them to feel good about the space they're in, y'know, so they can do something that's more natural. So simply, I think that at first we're looking for someone who's calm, receptive, and attentive.

"When actors are *too* friendly. Too friendly turns me off. You also have to understand, you may be the hundred and thirtieth of a hundred and fifty people I've seen today. By the time I see you, I want to get up and shake your hand, but I'm just *too tired*. So don't take it personally. If the director doesn't get up to say hello, it doesn't mean he doesn't like you."

> **TIP:** *If the director doesn't get up to say hello, it doesn't mean he doesn't like you.*

Listening Problems

So, there you are, checking out the space and trying to take focus, and suddenly, out of the maelstrom of activity in the back of the room, a tall dude in a baseball cap with an English accent is talking to you. It's the director! He's just gotten off the phone about a film deal he's been trying to close, and now he's turned his attention to you. And he's giving you key instructions about the scene you're about to play.

It's time to listen, and I mean really listen.

I can't tell you how many actors I've seen blow auditions by not listening.

Here's why: The director may throw you a curve. Be ready for it. He could have a different interpretation of the scene than you do, or may be experimenting with a new idea, and will ask you to play it differently. Or you both may be on the same page but the director may decide to push you in a different direction *just to see if you can take direction.*

Listen.

As George Roux relates, "I tell somebody to do something different and they'll do the take the exact same way! I want to ask them, 'Are your ears painted on?'"

> **TIP:** *The director may decide to push you in a different direction just to see how you handle it.*

Danny Levinson equates listening with understanding. "Understanding means really listening to what the director's saying. A lot of times people are nervous. So they want to ask a quick question because they're just nervous. Be a good listener in a casting session. If you have a question, ask it, but listen to what the director is saying. Take a deep breath and let it sink in, then do the scene. . . . *I* try to be a good listener when I'm casting. So, I ask questions and I listen to what they're saying, because it's my job to get inside the actor so I can help manipulate him or her to do what I want to do."

There are other situations that you may encounter. You may have made the wrong choice and the director is kind enough to try to nudge you onto the right track. Or, five minutes ago, while you were sitting outside, the agency rewrote a pivotal moment in the script. Surprise!

Beyond seeing how an actor takes direction, the director may have a hidden agenda that's actually in your favor, and you may not realize it. It's a situation that runs counter to my caveat about being too "selly" or overdoing a line. Michael Norman explains:

"I've learned to make sure that I do have takes that I like on the tape, but also, takes that are, let's say, a little 'more friendly' than I would like. That's because clients are so unsophisticated. And one thing that actors should remember is that you're not only doing this for the guys in the room, but at the end of the day, the tape is going to go to a client, and so I've learned in my old age to get performances that I know—if I really like this person—that I know will help. If a director says, 'Okay, we love what you're doing. Do one really over-the-top friendly now.' What they're trying to do is get something in their hip pocket that they can use to sell this actor to the client. This is increasingly becoming a big hill that the creative team and the director have to climb to get something past the client—who generally is fairly unsophisticated about what we do. . . . So I think that doing a take that maybe is a little pushed or a little forced, or really steps on a product line, or something a little more than an actor might feel comfortable doing—a lot of times that's done because, if we have to, we'll use that to sell the client. But then we'll go back and do what *we* really like when we shoot it."

Danny Levinson says, "If you like somebody, yeah, go ahead and cover it a few different ways. If you like somebody and you know they can do it the way you want them to do it but slightly different than what the client is going to want (but you want to do it both ways on the set), then certainly, getting the reading that you think the client will be more attracted to *and* the one that you want is a good way of going about it."

Listen and stay flexible. Realize that one of the things the director is doing is checking you out to see how you handle changes under pressure. *Most commercial shoots last only one day.* He wants to know that you can deal with adversity on the set.

So many times I've heard directors say something like, "That lady's really got something special going on, but I could never work with her. She doesn't take direction very well." In other words, she didn't listen.

How to Listen

Here's the best thing you can do to get over your nerves and begin listening: Once you come in and you've scoped out the room, *create a dialogue with the director*. A dialogue causes you to start *working* with the director. And once that relationship starts, you'll be listening. You'll be working instead of worrying about all the other distractions in the room.

Want to know a secret? Confident actors always ask questions.

New people are afraid to ask questions, and that's how we very quickly separate them from the pros. They make two big mistakes in callbacks that hinder their ability to listen and perform.

One is that when they come into the room and sit down, they assume that they're going to do the same thing they did last time. Before they begin, they strike out by *not* asking, "What is it that you'd like me to do?" Don't ever assume. Just ask and you'll have begun your dialogue with the director.

> **TIP:** *First thing: Create a dialogue with the director.*

Now here comes the dangerous part. After he sees what you've done, the director may say, "Try it sexy," or, "Do it funny," or something vague like that. The bad actor says the most dangerous word in show business: "Okay."

If you say okay, then you'll give the director exactly what he wanted, but the problem is you won't really know what he wanted because *you didn't let him explain it.* As soon as somebody gives direction, the actor's next job is to ask, "What do you mean? Do you mean like this?"

You've got to help the director help you. Directors know what they want; they often don't know how to tell actors how to get there. *"Do it funny?"* Well, there are all kinds of funny, so you need to really try to work with the director—not in a defensive way but in a way that helps you do *your* kind of funny. So you ask, "Funny like this or like that?" Now you're paying attention, you're listening. As you're giving him choices, he's *clarifying* his direction, you're both reaching a point of collaboration, which causes the director to start thinking, "I can work with this person."

So, what are legitimate questions an actor can ask a director? Here are two directors' takes on the subject:

"Sometimes people ask, 'What's the concept of this commercial?' and that would be fine to ask. I think that so much about doing a good performance is where your head's at—and that means being well informed about what you're doing and what's your motivation. Because time is of the essence, you don't want to ask *too* many questions. But you could still ask some pertinent questions like, 'Is this me talking to a friend or am I talking to the camera?' or, 'Where should my eye line be?' or, 'Am I really angry in this, or am I an amused, cynical character?' Questions like that are legitimate.

"If you're not sure about the concept, you could ask about the concept, absolutely. If you ask too many specific questions, it maybe looks like you're trying too hard. But, if it's a difficult concept and you don't ask a question and you don't know what you're doing, then you're sort of shortchanging yourself."

Making it into a callback gives you the right to ask *reasonable* questions. Just don't go overboard with the content and the number of questions because that only leads to creating bad thoughts with the ad people on the other side of the room. Thoughts like, "He's a very confused, uncomfortable dork who asks too many damn questions." You'll feel the room get chilly very quickly.

> **TIP:** *Asking reasonable questions helps you listen.*

Respect for You

Some ad agency people don't know how to behave because they're inexperienced or have big egos, and they can be curt or even rude. I apologize for them. It's inexcusable, but if someone says something that bothers you, don't feed into it. You must let it roll off your back.

Remember, *the director is the only person who should give you direction.* If an agency person starts putting his two cents in without clearing it with the director, turn your attention to the director and listen to him or her only. Agency people ought to know this rule, but every once in awhile somebody will pop off with a suggestion. Don't get confused; look to the director. If necessary, ask him, "Is that what you want me to do?"

> **TIP:** *The director is the only person who should give you direction.*

Also, nobody can tell you to do something you don't want to do. Be honest with your feelings and tell the person you'd feel uncomfortable doing it.

Rarely, somebody may say something to you that's really out of line, and you may want to tell him to stuff it, but be extremely careful how you handle yourself. I've seen a few actors get tweaked about a comment made to them, but thankfully, every one of them kept their composure. That's a good thing to remember because you always want to live to fight another day. You may get called by that agency again when they have a different director and you'll have a fresh opportunity to show off your stuff. Your best bet is to wait, and later complain to the casting director, your agent, or, ultimately, the union. Let them take care of it.

> **TIP:** *If someone says something that bothers you, keep your composure. Live to fight another day.*

On the Mark: Good Advice from Directors

Good directors become great directors because they all have one goal in mind: To produce the most exceptional commercial they possibly can with the resources they're given. They set very high standards and they expect you to share their values. The callback is their testing ground, their crucible. How do they work? What do they want? What do they feel?

In their own words, here's a look into the minds of some veteran directors:

Nicholas Barker brings a gift for humor, English sensibility and a compassion for actors to everything he directs:

"I'm fairly aware of the fact that the whole casting process for talent in the advertising world is a *brutal* sausage machine. And it's one that means that the talent is sort of demoralized before they've even started their performance. So that whole ritual of driving to the casting session, parking, signing in, and waiting conspires to make people miserable and demoralized. What I do as a director is I always—whatever happens—like my talent to leave my casting studio with their dignity intact. I always get them to do everything at least twice. And I'll always try to put them at ease and be sufficiently courteous so that they can give me a half-decent performance.

"It's the job of the talent to enable the director to start the casting session as quickly as possible. So a crucial quality is the ability to listen. If you have a tendency to be nervous and not listen, then you're not going to get very far in advertising auditions. There is absolutely no substitute for that one simple quality.

"Don't rip up the script on the first read, but certainly do something to make the script your own. The actor can, in the first instance, give the director what he wants, but just add in a few little things, personalize it, to make it just a little more interesting. And if he gets any feedback, of pleasure, then give more.

"The next crucial bit of advice from this English director is *never show off* in the session. Don't show off during the slate. Don't draw attention to yourself by being a smart aleck. Don't try and humor the agency or the casting director. *Everybody's* trying to do that. The way to get noticed is to draw attention to yourself by being quiet, highly attentive, and charming. If you quietly communicate that quality, people will notice you.

"Never try to take up too much of the director's time. He wants to assess your performance as quickly as possible and then get you out of there. And if you're good, he's going to be thrilled. So don't feel that, by spinning it out, you'll in any way increase your chances of getting the job. On the contrary, you probably reduce your chances.

"For a lot of actors, particularly actors who are more seasoned, who've done quite a few commercials, there's a danger that they gain jobs by being slick and professional, but without really giving of themselves. And what I often say to my talent is, 'If we get this right'—if we have a really good script—I'll say, 'it's sad but true, but this is probably the most famous thing you're ever going to do. In which case, let's make it awesome.' The point is, there are some moments in some of my commercials that are really, really memorable because I've worked with the talent and together, we've found ways of communicating painfully comedic little moments that are difficult to forget. There are lots of directors out there who desperately want help, directors who haven't got two ideas to rub together and are waiting for the talent to show them how the scene can be played.

"What a performance director really wants more than anything else is a precision instrument. It is so thrilling. It's like driving the most perfectly powerful, responsive car to be able to direct a really finely tuned actor."

Michael Norman believes it's more organic to have actors discover a performance rather than tell them exactly what to do:

"For me, especially when it comes to dialogue or monologue commercials, the hardest day of the shoot is the callback. I'm the most nervous on that day. [Nervous] that I'll find somebody good, that's right for the part, or that there's going to be a big battle at the end of that day with the agency, or maybe the next morning with the client. Generally, with the people in the room (the agency) you can come to some decent agreement. But there's some horse trading that takes place that may make me lose my favorite, or a compromise that can make somebody that I really love fall out. But you go, 'Oh well, another day I'll work with them.'

"How do I like to work with actors at a callback? It definitely depends on the nature of the spot. You see, I've had the benefit of seeing the casting tape with these people on it. Obviously, if they're people I've chosen (as opposed to those the agency's chosen) then I've seen what they did—and usually remember what they did—and I want to see them kind of replicate that in a way. I might change the staging of it a little bit, even though there isn't much [flexibility] in a casting room; I want to see what they did . . . kind of reassure what they did in the initial casting and see if they can duplicate that. It's very interesting that some people have no clue what they did. It's rare, but occasionally there'll be some-one who did some little nuance or something and they can't get back there again.

"I don't want to give too much instruction in the beginning—not make them think about too much stuff, but reinforce what they did initially. Not talk it to death right off the bat, but let them do a take. Usually I like to say very little in the beginning other than introduce myself and say we remember you from the tape and we really like what you did. Then I'll say, 'Let's shoot the rehearsal. Let's don't rehearse it first, we'll just shoot it and then do something.' And I think that once they do a performance, then that gives us something to work off of.

"So, in other words, I'd never try to tell them exactly what to do. I would rather tell them a story about the situation they're in that might motivate what they might do. I don't think actors appreciate that, anyway. And I don't think that gives an organic performance, you know, to tell them something like, 'Say it like this.' Everyone has their own way of doing it, so I always shoot the rehearsal—unless it's something complicated that maybe for some staging reason we'd need to rehearse ahead of time. But, generally I let 'em do their take on it. I don't want to over-instruct them.

"Or, if I really like what they did and I don't have any real comment, I'll go, 'I really liked that. Let's do another one.' Because, y'know, something different is going to happen. And I think that kind of starts to free them to move a little bit with it. So that, by the second take, I've had the time to process what it is they're doing and then make a little adjustment. Let's say it's a testimonial and they're talking to camera, I may suggest something like, 'You don't have to nail the lens so much. Let's see the wheels turning like when you're talking to the someone; and you're trying to think of what to say—y'know, like when you're thinking out loud.' I'll offer suggestions like that (which is a general technical direction) as opposed to telling the actor exactly how to say a word."

Danny Levinson's method depends on trusting that actors can deliver, and trusting that he can make it happen:

"I cast more and more now by just talking to someone. I don't even give them the dialogue, I don't even play out the scene. I just talk to them to see if they're intelligent and can understand. Maybe I'll have 'em read it once if it's a very specific line; some client is going to want to see it. But outside of that, if it's just a scene and these people are doing something, I just talk to them. You got to remember, [between] the director and the actor, it's weird to walk up to someone and look them in the eye for a whole day and tell them what to do, what they should be feeling. It's not natural. So you've just got to connect with somebody. The director wants to know that he can just talk to you.

"Most times, if it's a dialogue spot, we'll read a version of it in the casting session. But if I know you're intelligent, I know you listen, and I know you understand, I'll get you there because that's what I do."

⑭ Oh, Behaave! The Seven Deadly Sins Actors Commit in Front of the Agency

The door swings open. The contestant is led in to stand under the bright lights in front of the omnipotent camera. Cue the music. Zoom in. It's time for another episode of "I Left My Brain Outside," the nutty, embarrassing, exasperating little show that agency people watch about three times a day.

This not-so-entertaining show always stars people who are clueless about where they really are. They think they're in an audition studio, they think this is all about *them*, but they're actually in *our office*. Yes, we're working, too, and when actors come in they've got to understand that even though they're only going to be in here for about three minutes, we'll be here all day. People really are invading our space, and that's why parts of this book have been geared towards giving you an appreciation for what the agency humans have to deal with. As you've surmised by now, all of us sitting back there are under a ton of pressure. Please respect that we're actually at work and you're in our office.

Most folks come in and do their job, and their headshots either end up on the Yes Pile or the No Pile. C'est la vie. But those starring in "I Left My Brain Outside" land in the No Pile because they've committed one of the following sins:

1. CELL PHONES AND PAGERS
Already mentioned that, right?

2. BAD-HAIR DAYS
The worst thing you can do is carry in smelly baggage from outside and create a bad impression from the moment you enter the room. Your dog

died and your wife ran away with a bass player, you were caught in traffic, you hate the part, or you hate your agent for sending you for parts you hate. No matter what, you've got to leave all that crap outside, because we'll sense it. Immediately.

Even worse, an actor will come in and be just downright adversarial in her demeanor, like we were the enemy or something. Maybe it came from a snub by someone outside (where it should've stayed), or she genuinely feels superior to all this commercial B.S. This actor doesn't even have to open her mouth—her attitude tells us something is wrong, and that just sets us up to expect the worst. Unless she can shake it off, she'll die because she'll poison her performance.

Hey, you're a special, gifted artist—okay, fine—but most people in the room don't care about all that. Prima-donna attitudes do not increase your chances of getting hired.

3. SCHMOOZING

Occasionally, a talent will come in who either knows the director because they've worked together before or because the director has specifically called the actor in. I've observed the true professionals in these situations, and here's why they're pros: They just say "Higoodtaseeya," and then they get on with the work. No schmoozing, no war stories, just focus—ask the director a good question about the part and go to work. If you're one of those lucky few that knows the director, don't waste his time, our time, and especially the short time you have in the room with chitchat. Just be friendly old you and get on with it.

When you come in, don't start overselling yourself, either, because nobody wants someone that's pushy. One sure way to lose a part is to play *to* the director or someone in the room you think is important. Come in, head for that chair or the spot, find the director, and start working. Show us that you're a working actor.

And finally, don't chat up the video operator. Unlike his function at the initial call, where he might have been running the show, the video operator in this situation is now just another piece of equipment for the director to use. He may tell you to scoot over in your chair to get you in frame or something like that, but your main focus should be on the director.

4. TERRITORY VIOLATIONS

This is our territory back here on our side of the room. Your territory is up there in front of the camera. Crossing the line can be risky. Occasionally, an actor will walk back to the table and shake hands with everybody. I know some people think that's a gesture designed to break the ice and get friendly, but it's not only a waste of time, it seems amateurish. Honestly, we don't really want to shake your hand or personally meet you. We're far more comfortable being the anonymous jury.

Plus, you're crashing into the sanctity of our space.

You'll probably notice a lot of snacks and things to nibble on sitting back there on our table. Unbelievably, I've had actors come back and take a handful of M&M's from my dish and not even say please. You can understand why this is risky behavior.

Don't come back and hand out flyers to your play, either. If the agency is from out of town, they'll be too tired to go out to a play. Afterward they're going to the hotel, have dinner, and crash.

Take stock of your territory and make it yours. Stay out of ours.

5. WARMING UP

What technique do you use to warm up for a scene? Method-acting techniques? Yoga? Feldenkrais? Panting? Whatever you use, please leave all those gyrations outside. We don't have the time—or the stomach—to witness them.

6. DISSING THE PRODUCT

You never *ever* want to insult the product! Even jokingly. We once saw an actor pick up the product and confide, "C'mon guys, tell me—does this shit really work?" Yes it did, but he didn't.

Michael Waters says: don't pee all over yourself about the product, either. Even if you actually use it, or shop there, or eat one, and you gush, "I love this stuff *so much*!!" it'll seem like you're trying to suck up to us.

7. NOT KNOWING WHEN IT'S OVER

A good guest knows when the party's over; why can't some actors?

You've heard this before: "Thanks, good job" or, "Well, thanks for coming in," or, "Yeah, that was good, I think I've seen plenty." Which means that the audition's over and it's time to go. If the director's put you through some paces, made you work, and had you read more than two times, then you should be pretty satisfied that you've had a darn good rip at it and it's time to go.

Don't wait until you have to get the hook.

On the other hand, if you've read once, maybe twice, and you hear, "Thanks for coming in," don't ask if you can read again. You won't get the chance, because the director has either decided he doesn't like you and he wants you out of there, or *he really likes you* and your headshot is about to move over to the Yes pile on our table.

Say "thanks" and go.

Don't ever stand around afterwards and say silly things like, "Hey, I'm appearing in *Streetcar* at the Actor's Zoo. Y'all oughta come and see it."

Go away!

However, when a director says to the casting director, "Look, can you have Michelle hang around for a minute?" that means he likes you enough to have you come back in and read with another actor. You know what to do. Relax, but stay focused. And try not to smile too openly.

And finally, here's a really good tip: Once you exit the studio, don't leave!

This happens a lot. After an actor exits the audition studio, the director and the agency confer and someone will pipe up, "You know, there was something about that girl that was really appealing and I think we missed it. Can we get her back in here for a minute and try directing her to do such and such?" The director says okay and sends the casting director out to the waiting area to find her. But too late—she's gone, headed for the car, thinking about what a bad job she did.

Another scenario is this: There's a gap in the call, or it's the end of the day, and there aren't any guys left to read with the lone girl. Dude, that could've been your second chance!

So. Hang around for a minute or two in the waiting area. I'm not saying camp out, but take a moment to make a phone call or freshen your makeup or something. You never know—you may get another shot.

TIP: *After your audition, hang around for a minute or two in the waiting area.*

⑮ Decision Time

The actors have left, the lights are cooling down, and now, the production company and the agency sit down to review their choices. This is the moment of truth. We can't leave until we've cast the commercial.

WHAT HAPPENS AFTER YOU'RE GONE

All day we've been making notes and stacking pictures in three piles: Yes, No, and "Ehh?" Now, the pictures begin to shift from pile to pile. As the Yes pile gets smaller, the arguments get more passionate. Time and again we'll replay the videotape to review performances and weigh them against our criteria. Back and forth we'll go, making a case for our picks. Who has the most powerful vote? If it's an experienced agency and a big-time director, the director has a slight edge. If it's an inexperienced agency, the director holds sway.

No matter who says what, ultimately it will be the director who stands on the set whispering into an actor's ear. So, besides an actor having the right look or delivering a dynamite performance—even besides the X-factor—the director is going to base his decision on another very important observation: How will you handle the pressure of the shoot? On the set you become another part of a large puzzle the director is trying to assemble. That's why Michael Norman says, "You want to feel that there's a certain steadiness to the person, I guess, in terms of their temperament and self-confidence. You want a sense that 'this person can play well with the other kids.' Our business is all about that in every job category because, for instance, the cameraman is going to ask you to 'look this way, feel the light,' or I'm going to give you all this little staging stuff, or makeup is going to be coming in between takes, and stuff like that. And so you want somebody who's real hard to frustrate. Everybody [the crew] is going to come at the actor with these little questions, so I want someone who's difficult to fluster.

"I've learned to be sensitive to whether a person is going to have a lot of weird requirements. Certainly you want to make them comfortable and not make them do something they wouldn't normally do, but I look for the subtle little things that tell me this is someone that can *collaborate,* not only with me, but with the crew's requirements, which are technical."

Finally the Yes pile shrinks and we come to consensus. We'll choose three actors for each part: One first choice and two backups. The first choice is the one everyone believes in, but the two backups have to be very, very close seconds, because chances are that the client could like one of the backups better than the first choice, and we've got to be very comfortable with that actor.

Next day, the three choices are presented to the client, preferably in person, but often the tape will be FedExed overnight. It used to be a lot easier to sell our choices, but in recent years, the job has gotten tougher. If the agency painted a strong picture of the character weeks ago at the agency's presentation and the impression stayed in the client's mind, then we stand a good chance of selling our favorite choice for the part. But things change over the course of time, including the minds of clients. In today's take-charge climate of Corporate America, clients have become self-anointed talent scouts and casting experts. And that's when the agency relies on the strength of the director's opinion and reasoning. Generally, clients will defer to his recommendations.

Whew. Done. Cast.

The lead actor is immediately put "on availability," and one of the two backups is held as the first alternate in the event that the lead actor cannot make the shoot. If you are chosen as an alternate, keep your schedule open. As you know, sometimes the understudy becomes the lead.

SO YOU DIDN'T BOOK THE JOB

Boo hoo! The phone didn't ring the next day. "Damn!" you're thinking. "I did my homework. I figured out the concept. I knew who I was in that commercial. I came in ready to work. I nailed it! What did I do wrong?"

If you honestly, truly feel you did everything right, you're probably right, so don't beat yourself up. Don't take it personally, because despite the obvious reasons you didn't get cast, remember—there are a hundred others that have nothing to do with you: You could have been called in because the director is checking you out for something else he has in mind, or the client may have stepped into the agency's business and demanded a certain type, or . . . or, maybe it just wasn't your day. Michael Norman says, "One thing actors should understand is that if they don't get the part, there're *so* many reasons why. Demographics are such a big reason when an actor doesn't get a part. Or they're wrong for it on so many levels that they shouldn't feel bad at all."

Every time you walk into that room there will be a new group of people to win over. People with different criteria, different fears, and different attitudes. My friends, you can't be everything to everybody. Remember, the ad factory spews out commercials in many different sizes and colors every day, and each one offers different roles to play. You won't be right for every one, but you'll get the ones that are right for you.

You may take some solace in Danny Levinson's point of view:

"I'm a director. By my nature, I'm a Jewish guy from New York. I like the way certain types of men look, I like the way certain types of women look, that's just the way *I* am. And you know what, there's a million directors like me, and everybody likes something different, *so there is an actor for every director!* I have my likes, my dislikes; I like brunettes, not blondes, generally speaking. So on any given day you may not get cast for a hundred different reasons. And you shouldn't take it personally."

That's why you have to be yourself, and you'll find your niche. Or rather, the niche will find you. . . . The niche will find *you*."

16 Congratulations, You Got the Part

Sweet! You've booked a job. All of your hard work is about to be paid off with one of the coolest, most fascinating, difficult, nerve-wracking, fun experiences you could ever have. The best advice I can pass along from working actors is to get a good night's sleep. The day starts early and goes on forever.

ON THE SHOOT

Every commercial shoot takes on a life of its own, so I'm not going to take up much space here attempting to describe all the nuances. Besides, this is a book about auditioning, and hopefully it's helped you get this far.

Nonetheless, here are a few things that should be helpful:

Most commercial shoots take only one day, maybe two, to complete.

When you're notified that you've been booked, you'll be given directions to the studio or the location and the phone number of someone from the production company. If you're running late or have an emergency on shoot day, let your agent handle it first. In the event of a genuine screaming emergency, call the production-company number.

When you arrive, *don't* look for the director. He or she's too busy and will rarely come to greet you. Today, you are only one cog in a giant machine the director is trying to run. Ask for the first-assistant director (the first-AD), or the production company or agency producer. One of them will help you get situated and most likely take you to the wardrobe/stylist people.

Since I'm a former actor, I always try to make a point of seeking out the talent to say "hi" and fill them in about what's going on with the shoot and make them feel at ease. Personally, I'm genuinely happy to finally meet the people we've hired 'cause I know how much they've had to go through to get here. I'm a nice guy, but don't expect this kind of welcome wagon from everybody.

Maybe it comes from nerves, but every once in awhile an actor will say, "Y'know, they call me 'One-Take Johnson,'" or, "'One-Take Gina.'" You shouldn't worry about being one-take anybody because that's just going to put too much pressure on yourself. Relax. They've got a lot of film, an infinite amount of pixels, the director's got some ideas, and you don't have to worry about nailing it in one take. Unless you're the stuntperson.

Directors have their own unique ways of running things on their set. They each have a style that they believe helps them handle the mayhem and do better work. For instance, before he became an incredible still photographer and later a fine director, Norman Seeff was a surgeon in South Africa. When shooting intimate one-on-one dialogue scenes I've seen him seal off the shooting area with drapes to create the atmosphere of an operating room. It's quite effective. Stu Hagman got so tired of shouting over the din of his crew that he got one of those "Mr. Microphones" with the remote speaker. His disembodied voice of God emanates from the middle of his set, and you have to get used to it.

Remember that you were hired because you were already 75 percent "there" with your performance at the callback, so don't change anything unless you're told to do so. Have your lines memorized but don't lock yourself in too much because, believe me, the script probably changed once again. The director will probably have some different ideas up his sleeve, too, and they may be 180 degrees counter to your expectations. Anything can happen. Do everything you can to stay loose but stay focused, because I'm telling you, even if you have a teeny tiny part, once you get in front of the camera, you'll quickly discover that it's like trying to assemble a fine Swiss watch in the middle of a tornado.

Here's one director's advice: "If it's a storytelling commercial that has no dialogue, there's almost no way to be prepared for that. (We're going to shoot in such little snippets that it's easier to have instantaneous motivation from somebody who's probably more physical than anything else.) But when it comes to dialogue, learning a script is a dangerous thing to do before a shoot day, because, invariably, it's going to change. So just get a good night's sleep or whatever. You should always ask if you can take the script, [and if you do] don't over-study it because the likelihood is that you're going to show up the next morning and in make-up they're going to show you a script that's got juuust enough different stuff that it's going to make you crazy.

"We generally don't shoot anything all the way through the script, anyway. But if we do try to do that and have trouble, we always know where we can pick up sections of it. I like to put giant cue cards all around the set, near camera, so that in between takes actors can check the script. And what it helps *me* do is that I can point to a line or a section [and we'll work on it]. If it's possible—and this might be asking too much, but you could feel this out with the AD when you get there in the morning—ask if there's a way to get a big script up somewhere. I think that's very helpful."

There're two main people you should listen to when you're in front of the camera. The director of photography (the DP) has positioned the camera, lit the scene, and framed the shot so he may give you information about your body position and framing. The director will tell you everything else. If you have any questions about anything ask him or her. Don't listen to comments from strange voices behind the camera over in a place called "video village." That's the area in front of the playback monitors set aside for the agency and the client to park their butts.

Danny Levinson has some suggestions on how to get along on a set. "Just be normal. Be yourself. A lot of times you're not going to see the director greet you on the set because either the director is busy, or he has no confidence so he doesn't want to come talk to you, or you're a good-looking girl and he may start sweating if he talks to you, or you're a guy and he gets upset by good-looking guys—who knows! Or, he may come right up to you in the morning. It's really hard for actors because you come on, you're the star of the show, and you get all the attention that day from somebody that you don't even know. It's a weird thing. That's why you have to be yourself, so you can roll and be fluid. Keep your ears open, keep your eyes open. If you don't know something, ask. They may think you're just charmingly naïve.

"You'll find that the most successful commercial actors, for the most part, are the ones who can have a normal conversation away from the camera. They're just *people*."

Well, you finally made it. The DP barks a final order to the grips about adjusting a light and tells you that the camera is going to swing towards you just so and then stop. He holds a light meter under your chin and checks his exposure. The camera operator runs a measuring tape out to double-check his focal length. A girl with purple hair leans in and dusts more powder on your face. The director kneels down next to you and gives you a reassuring word or two.

"Just focus on what you have to do and listen to me. Ready?"

"Quiet, please."

The room settles down.

"Roll camera."

"Speed."

"Marker."

"Aaand *action!*"

17 Resources—make it Your Business to Know Our Business

Smart actors are always working on the business of acting, and they continue to look for ways to get seen or heard. Business-savvy actors often ask if it's helpful to send their headshots and tapes to ad agencies and production companies. I wish I could tell you it's a great way to be remembered, but it's not. Those materials just get thrown away. Agency and production people just toss your stuff in the trash because they're so busy creating and managing advertising that they don't have time to pay attention to actors. That's why casting directors were created, and they should be the focus of your personal advertising campaign. As a matter of fact, you could take some of the information from Advertising 101 and create a campaign for yourself.

> **TIP:** *Sending headshots and tapes to agency personnel is a waste of time.*

Your best course of action is to stay up on current trends in advertising and be aware of movers and shakers in the commercial production arena, as well as the agencies. Keep abreast of our side of the business by reading our "trades," and you'll enjoy a more comfortable position at auditions because you'll know *even more* than the actor sitting next to you. Give yourself an edge. There are some excellent industry publications available and most have Web sites that offer online subscriptions. In addition to some other helpful sites, I've also included those sites mentioned earlier in the book.

Before you check these out, I invite you to visit my Web site at *www.howtoaudition.com*. I'll be keeping track of helpful resources and new Web sites for commercial actors, and updating new information and trends in the commercial business. You'll also be able to e-mail your questions, concerns, good news, and any helpful audition tips you'd like to share. And when I'm out speaking, I'll post the towns and schools where I'll be appearing and the dates when I'll be there.

Okay. Here are Web sites and publications that every commercial actor should keep abreast of:

AdWeek is a weekly subscription-based print and electronic magazine covering everything in the business of advertising, from accounts in review, to people in the business, employment, awards, and more. It features regionalized editions. You can go to their site and get an overview of the news for free. Go to *www.adweek.com.*

Advertising Age is a weekly subscription print and electronic magazine featuring reports and breaking news for the marketing and advertising industry. Go to *www.adage.com.*

Far more edgy than the previous two, *Creativity* magazine is a monthly newspaper that seeks out new viewpoints, and highlights creative executions that push the limits of advertising. It offers reviews and critiques of TV commercials. Subscribe at *www.adcritic.com.*

Shoot Magazine is the font of information for the commercial production industry. It highlights directors and production companies, trends, new technology, and agency creatives. Visit them at *www.shootonline.com.* You can subscribe on a month-to-month basis by contacting them at: 5055 Wilshire Boulevard, Los Angeles, CA 90036. Phone: (323) 525-2262 or (800) 745-8922.

'boards magazine is an online magazine covering all the international business of commercial production. Features articles, screening room, and more. Visit *www.boardsmag.com.*

For a monthly overview of the most interesting new contributions to U.K. television advertising, visit *Xtreme New Commercials* at *www.xnc.co.uk.*

Earlier in the book I suggested some ways to check out commercial directors. Here's that information again:

A good place to start is the *Directors Guild of America* at *www.dga.org.* They have a fairly straightforward list of directors.

The *411 Directories* are an industry resource for everything from animal wranglers to directors. They have an East Coast and a Left Coast site. Go to either *www.la411.com* or *www.newyork411.com* and click on "Production Companies and Ad Agencies." You can surf the production companies and, in most cases, link to their sites. You'll find directors on their sites.

To find directors, view reels, and look at current commercials, there's *CreativeChannel*, at *www.fastchannel.com/creativechannel*. It's a really great site for just about everything and is fee based.

Aforementioned *AdCritic* (*www.adcritic.com*) is a subscription site, but it's really worth it. They are all about current TV commercials, directors, and production companies.

The Source Maythenyi is also a top-notch site for directors and commercials. It's also fee based. Go to *www.sourcetv.com*.

I've mentioned acting coach Bernard Hiller, and you should visit his Web site. Although Bernard's studio is located in Los Angeles, his site provides information on his out-of-town seminars plus details on the valuable classes he teaches. Check it out at *www.bernardhiller.com*.

The Last World

You know, it really is cool to be sitting on the couch and a TV commercial comes on and you go, "Hey! That's my spot!" Whether you wrote it, directed it, or especially, appeared in it, seeing your work on air at the same time millions of other people are watching is a hit.

I wrote this book so that possibly, you can enjoy that moment, too.

Hopefully the message of this book has been more encouraging than discouraging. I truly feel for actors. It's a tough business.

Hang in there. Good luck. I'll be looking for you from my side of the room.

Acknowledgements

I had a lot of fun writing this book. I had a lot of help writing it, too. Without question, I couldn't have done it without the incredible support and encouragement of my wife, Cora Lea, and the quiet, positive energy put out by our buddies Bunny, Mutt, and Carmel.

When I was looking for a publisher, Allworth Press asked me if I was seeking a home for my book and I couldn't have found a more responsive and professional team to work with. Publisher Tad Crawford, editor Nicole Potter-Talling, editor Jessica Rozler, and the rest of the Allworth staff have definitely made a nice home for me.

Thanks to:

Every actor who's ever auditioned for me.

Actor Bernard Hiller, who didn't know it at the time, but by allowing me to be a guest speaker/teacher at his audition class, helped lay the groundwork for this book.

Contributing actors Chris Dollard, Troy Evans, and Kevin John Reilly. Also, Hector Elizondo, Doug Johnson, Joe Spano, Michael Leibert, and all the other troopers I've had the pleasure to work with either on stage, on camera, or in my commercials. You've taught me a lot.

Actor Jim McEachin, for his enthusiasm and encouragement.

Actor Sheldon Feldner, who, one chardonnay-fueled evening at the old Blarney Stone in North Hollywood way back when, convinced me that I would be a better writer than an actor.

Directors George Roux, Michael Norman, and Danny Levinson, for their words and wisdom. Special thanks to director Nicholas Barker, who contributed to this book from the U.K. And to the great directors I've worked with in years gone by.

Producers Joe Rein and Elissa Singstock, who have saved my ass on numerous occasions. And producers Michael Waters and Sam Penfield, who provided valuable insights and help.

Legendary L.A. casting directors Dorothy Kelly and Susie Kittleson, two wonderful women who have seen it all and shared their knowledge.

My mentor, and Clio Hall of Fame Creative Director, Howie Cohen.

Art director Mardel Monet, who's not only my good friend and a former coworker, but also the storyboard artist for the MegaPhone ad.

Storyboard artist Marcus Endean, who is truly one of the most generous people I've ever met, not to mention a terrific talent. He illustrated the individual storyboard frames and the Bodacious commercial.

Good friend Christine Aguilar, who lent me the book that showed me how to get published.

Kim Guggenheim, Esq., who is a great guy to have in your corner.

My pals at Dragonfly Design: Peter Godefroy, Jesse Cooper, and Aaron Trask, who helped me pull together the final art.

And last but not least, LuLu and Dick Schumacher, who have always been there for me.

Thank you all.

The End

Index

Books from Allworth Press

Allworth Press is an imprint of Allworth Communications, Inc. Selected titles are listed below.

Acting—Advanced Techniques for the Actor, Director, and Teacher
by Terry Schreiber (paperback, 6 × 9, 256 pages, $19.95)

Improv for Actors
by Dan Diggles (paperback, 6 × 9, 246 pages, $19.95)

Movement for Actors
edited by Nicole Potter (paperback, 6 × 9, 288 pages, $19.95)

Acting That Matters
by Barry Pineo (paperback, 6 × 9, 240 pages, $16.95)

The Art of Auditioning
by Rob Decina (paperback, 6 × 9, 224 pages, $19.95)

An Actor's Guide—Making It in New York City
by Glenn Alterman (paperback, 6 × 9, 288 pages, $19.95)

Creating Your Own Monologue, Second Edition
by Glenn Alterman (paperback, 6 × 9, 256 pages, $19.95)

Promoting Your Acting Career, Second Edition
by Glenn Alterman (paperback, 6 × 9, 224 pages, $19.95)

The Best Things Ever Said in the Dark:
The Wisest, Wittiest, Most Provocative Quotations from the Movies
by Bruce Adamson (hardcover, 7 1/2 × 7 1/2, 144 pages, $14.95)

Acting for Film
by Cathy Haase (paperback, 6 × 9, 240 pages, $19.95)

Technical Film and TV for Nontechnical People
by Drew Campbell (paperback, 6 × 9, 256 pages, $19.95)

The Health and Safety Guide for Film, TV and Theater
by Monona Rossol (paperback, 6 × 9, 256 pages, $19.95)

Please write to request our free catalog. To order by credit card, call 1-800-491-2808 or send a check or money order to Allworth Press, 10 East 23rd Street, Suite 510, New York, NY 10010. Include $5 for shipping and handling for the first book ordered and $1 for each additional book. Ten dollars plus $1 for each additional book if ordering from Canada. New York State residents must add sales tax.

To see our complete catalog on the World Wide Web, or to order online, you can find us at
www.allworth.com.